ASTROLOGY

JANIS HUNTLEY has been a practising astrologer for over 30 years. In addition to her extensive writing experience, which includes star sign columns and producing astrological articles for popular women's magazines and the media, she is a lecturer, teacher and consultant in the subject. She is the author of *Astrological Voids* and *The Complete Illustrated Guide to Astrology* which are also published by Element Books.

THE SERIES

New Perspectives provide attractive and accessible introductions to a comprehensive range of mind, body and spirit topics. Beautifully designed and illustrated, these practical books are written by experts in each subject.

Titles in the series include:

ASTROLOGY
by Janis Huntley

BUDDHISM
by John Snelling

CHAKRAS
by Naomi Ozaniec

COLOUR THERAPY
by Pauline Wills

CRYSTAL THERAPY
by Stephanie Harrison & Tim Harrison

HERBAL REMEDIES
by Vicki Pitman

I CHING
by Stephen Karcher

NUTRITIONAL THERAPY
by Jeannette Ewin

RUNES
by Bernard King

SHAMANISM
by Nevill Drury

TAI CHI
by Paul Crompton

YOGA
by Howard Kent

New Perspectives

ASTROLOGY

An Introductory Guide to the Influence of the Stars on your Life

JANIS HUNTLEY

ELEMENT

Shaftesbury, Dorset • Boston, Massachusetts
Melbourne, Victoria

© Element Books Limited 2000
Text © Janis Huntley 1990, 2000

First published as *The Elements of Astrology* in 1990 by
Element Books Limited

This revised edition first published in Great Britain in 2000 by
Element Books Limited, Shaftesbury, Dorset SP7 8BP

Published in the USA in 2000 by
Element Books, Inc.
160 North Washington Street,
Boston, MA 02114

Published in Australia in 2000 by
Element Books and distributed by
Penguin Australia Limited,
487 Maroondah Highway, Ringwood,
Victoria 3134

Designed for Element Books Limited by
Design Revolution, Queens Park Villa,
30 West Drive, Brighton, East Sussex BN2 2GE

ELEMENT BOOKS LIMITED
Editorial Director: Sarah Sutton
Project Editor: Kelly Wakely
Commissioning Editor: Grace Cheetham
Production Director: Roger Lane

DESIGN REVOLUTION
Editorial Director: Ian Whitelaw
Art Director: Lindsey Johns
Project Editor: Nicola Hodgson
Editor: Susie Behar
Designer: Vanessa Good

Printed and bound in Great Britain by
Bemrose Security Printing, Derby

British Library Cataloguing in Publication
Data available

Library of Congress Cataloging in Publication
Data available

ISBN 1-86204-666-2

CONTENTS

FOREWORD

I have always been baffled by the aura of complexity and mystery which surrounds the issue of learning astrology. 'I couldn't possibly absorb all that!' or 'I'd love to be able to work out a birth chart but it looks far too involved for me' are typical comments I have heard throughout the many years of my teaching experience in astrology.

It's not surprising, however, when you glance at some of the textbooks available on the subject to find that few of them cater for the average person, who would like to learn about astrology for their own interest, rather than to study over a period of several years, take a diploma, and become a professional astrologer.

It is in this respect that my book differs. For those of you who would like to learn astrology without too much effort or mathematical genius, this book is indispensable. Using my own simple system of guidance, most students can construct a birth chart and understand the basic principles of interpretation very quickly. Much of the mathematical calculation has been eliminated, but for those that baulk at the minimal amount required, there are many excellent computer programs available which take care of all the hard work. The only details required are date, place and time of birth.

The main criterion in erecting a birth chart is the time of birth, but the precise moment of birth is not easily defined. Is it our first breath, or is it the actual moment we emerge from the womb? Interpretation is the most important consideration in astrology, and good interpretative readings do not depend upon precise mathematical calculations. It does not matter how long you take to learn astrology – after studying the nine chapters of this book, you will have a good outline of the basic principles of this fascinating subject. Good luck in your endeavours.

INTRODUCTION TO SIGNS AND PLANETS

CHAPTER ONE

In this first chapter I am going to introduce you to the basic tools of interpretative astrology, namely the twelve signs of the zodiac and the ten known planets of our solar system. In order for you to progress swiftly to erecting an individual's birth chart, it is vital that you learn thoroughly the natural sequence of the signs and planets, their astrological symbols, and a few important keywords of interpretation.

SIGNS OF THE ZODIAC

ARIES: The Ram (21 March to 19 April) Symbol: ♈

KEYWORD CHARACTERISTICS

Dominant, energetic, extroverted, impulsive, impatient, self-seeking, adventurous, argumentative, ardent, outspoken, hot-tempered.

APPEARANCE:

Irregular bold features. Angular face. Medium height. Often red or sandy-coloured hair with receding hairline in men.

RIGHT THE RAM SYMBOLIZES THE INDEPENDENCE AND PUSHINESS OF ARIES.

TAURUS: The Bull (20 April to 20 May) Symbol: ♉

KEYWORD CHARACTERISTICS

Steady, reliable, materialistic, stubborn, musical, plodding, practical, green-fingered, sturdy, domesticated, loyal.

APPEARANCE

Large, solid build. Square jaw. Thick curly hair, often dark. Short to medium height.

LEFT TAURUS SHARES THE QUALITIES OF STEADINESS AND STUBBORNESS WITH ITS SYMBOL, THE BULL.

GEMINI: The Twins (21 May to 21 June) Symbol: ♊

KEYWORD CHARACTERISTICS

Lively, versatile, highly strung, moody, communicative, jack of all trades, unemotional, unsympathetic, gesticulative, independent.

APPEARANCE

Medium height to tall, with slim build. Twinkling eyes. Long arms or legs. Expressive hands. Attractive features.

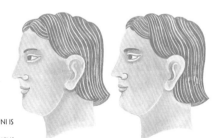

RIGHT THE VERSATILITY AND ADAPTABILITY OF GEMINI IS REPRESENTED IN THE DUAL IMAGE OF THE TWINS.

CANCER: The Crab (22 June to 22 July) Symbol: ♋

KEYWORD CHARACTERISTICS

Sensitive, protective, nurturing, clinging, sentimental, quiet, home loving, security orientated, sarcastic, reticent, kind.

APPEARANCE

Face either pale and round or sanguine and sharp. Blonde or black hair, usually sparse. Build plump and short.

LEO: The Lion (23 July to 22 August) Symbol: ♌

KEYWORD CHARACTERISTICS

Proud, egocentric, fun-loving, loud, bombastic, generous, lazy, determined, showy, theatrical, likeable, unrelenting, bossy.

APPEARANCE

Thick wavy, blonde or red hair drawn back from the face. Sunny expression. Females usually well-adorned. Height medium to tall, often corpulent.

VIRGO: The Virgin (23 August to 22 September) Symbol: ♍

KEYWORD CHARACTERISTICS

Analytical, conscientious, discerning, critical, cool, fussy, intelligent, communicative, organizing, retiring, diligent, restless, modest.

APPEARANCE

Medium to tall build. Men usually slim in youth. Females tend to be plump. Staring or studious expression. Often lively or talkative exterior.

LIBRA: The Scales (23 September to 22 October) Symbol: ♎

KEYWORD CHARACTERISTICS

Well-balanced, indecisive, fair, serene, self-absorbed, charming, polite, refined, lacking depth, sociable, impractical.

APPEARANCE

Medium to tall build. Prone to plumpness in later years. Attractive. Men often effeminate. Round or oval face. Sleek hair.

RIGHT EARTHY VIRGO CAN HAVE A RESTLESS AND LIVELY TEMPERAMENT.

SCORPIO: The Scorpion (23 October to 21 November) Symbol:

KEYWORD CHARACTERISTICS

Secretive, emotional, intense, highly-sexed, possessive, jealous, spiritual, penetrating, sharp, observant, determined, unshakeable, generous or stringent to a fault.

APPEARANCE

Square face. Deepset, or large round eyes which exude magnetism. Stocky build. Females curvaceous. Thick hair. Wide, straight mouth.

LEFT THE SCORPION WITH THE STING IN ITS TAIL SYMBOLIZES SCORPIO'S PASSIONATE AND JEALOUS NATURE.

10

SAGITTARIUS: The Archer
(22 November to 21 December) Symbol:

KEYWORD CHARACTERISTICS

Frank, blunt, outspoken, honest, chatty, knowledgeable, freedom seeking, restless, unreliable, changeable, optimistic, good-humoured, quick tempered.

APPEARANCE

Tall and slim, becoming larger with increasing years. Long, oval face. Lustrous, wavy, red or dark hair. Expressive eyes.

CAPRICORN: The Goat (22 December to 19 January) Symbol: ♑

KEYWORD CHARACTERISTICS

Cautious, shy, insecure, prudent, reliable, practical, down-to-earth, ambitious, status-seeking, reserved, sensuous, hard-working.

APPEARANCE

Small, slim or bony frame. Thin fine hair, usually dark. Retain youthful appearance into old age. Serious expression.

AQUARIUS: The Water Carrier
(20 January to 18 February) Symbol: ♒

KEYWORD CHARACTERISTICS

Outgoing, friendly, detached, humanitarian, impersonal, self-opinionated, eccentric, clever, ingenious, talented, unemotional.

APPEARANCE

Attractive, even features. Square-set jaw, or pronounced chin. Usually dark-haired. Tall and slim in youth.

PISCES: The Fishes
(19 February to 20 March) Symbol: ♓

ABOVE ECCENTRICITY AND INVENTIVENESS ARE TWO QUALITIES ASSOCIATED WITH AQUARIANS.

KEYWORD CHARACTERISTICS

Dreamy, emotional, sensitive, shy, confused, escapist, introverted, artistic, vague, immoral, adaptable, muddle-headed, moody.

APPEARANCE

Build, anything from extremely tall to extremely short. Large, protuberant or attractive eyes. Tendency to plumpness. Something untidy or chaotic about outer demeanour.

It is important to note that the dates given for the change of signs are only approximate, and can vary by as much as two whole days in any given year. In chapter 3 you will learn how to read an astrological ephemeris, which gives exact times and dates when the Sun and other planets change sign.

LEFT THE VAGUENESS OF PISCEANS IS REPRESENTED BY THE IMAGE OF TWO FISH SWIMMING IN OPPOSITE DIRECTIONS.

THE PLANETS

The planets are undoubtedly the most important tools of astrological interpretation. Each of the ten planets commonly used in astrology possesses its own unique characteristics, and is designated to rule one particular sign of the zodiac. However, as you may already have deduced, there are only ten planets to go round the 12 signs. Therefore the two planets Venus and Mercury hold the enviable task of ruling two signs of the zodiac each.

Sun	☉	Rules Leo
Moon	☽	Rules Cancer
Mercury	☿	Rules Gemini and Virgo
Venus	♀	Rules Taurus and Libra
Mars	♂	Rules Aries
Jupiter	♃	Rules Sagittarius
Saturn	♄	Rules Capricorn
Uranus	♅	Rules Aquarius
Neptune	♆	Rules Pisces
Pluto	♇	Rules Scorpio

12

Each of the above planets takes a certain length of time to circle around the Earth and encompass the 12 signs of the zodiac. The Moon, which is the fastest-moving planet, takes only 28 days to orbit the earth and spends approximately two and a half days in one sign of the zodiac, whereas Pluto the outermost planet can spend up to 30 years in one sign alone.

It is for this reason that the planets are divided into three distinct divisions:

Sun
Moon
Mercury
Venus
} The first five planets move relatively swiftly and are therefore regarded as PERSONAL planets.

Jupiter
Saturn
} These move more slowly and are regarded as the two MIDDLE planets.

Uranus
Neptune
Pluto
} Extremely slow moving, these are the three outer planets, which tend to be more generational in effect.

Each planet represents a certain method of expressing ourselves:

13

The SUN is our ego, our individuality, the essential core of our whole character. It relates to how we view ourselves on an inner level. For example: Do you regard yourself as confident, impulsive and brash as the Sun in Aries would, or do you see yourself as being cautious, shy, lacking in confidence, as is more typical of the Sun in Capricorn?

ABOVE THE TEN PLANETS EACH RULE A DIFFERENT SIGN OF THE ZODIAC, WITH MERCURY AND VENUS RULING TWO SIGNS.

The MOON represents our emotions, feelings, responses and habits, and is very important in the birth charts of children. For example: Do you respond to a stressful situation with sensitivity, tears and shyness, as would a person with Moon in Pisces, or would you analyse the situation and talk matters over in the typical manner of somebody who has the Moon in Virgo or Gemini?

MERCURY rules the manner in which we communicate, through speech, thought, learning or writing. It is strongly associated with the mind. For example: Do you talk in a forthright, open manner, as the person with Mercury in Sagittarius does, or are you more of a 'deep thinker' than a conversationalist like somebody with Mercury in Scorpio?

VENUS indicates how we love, what we appreciate and value, our strivings for perfection and harmony. For example: Do you love protectively, nurturingly, caringly, and value your home, as would someone with Venus in Cancer, or do you tend to love detachedly at a distance, perhaps valuing companionship and communication more than romance, like the person with Venus in Aquarius?

MARS rules the amount of energy and drive we possess, our sexuality, aggressive tendencies, and self-seeking characteristics. For example: Is much of your energy directed towards materialism, or nature conservation as would be typical of the person with Mars in Taurus, or is your energy diverse, changeable, emotionally unstable, or confused, as could occur with Mars in Pisces?

JUPITER represents the manner in which we expand ourselves. It is also indicative of our religious and philosophical beliefs. This planet can make us feel on top of the world. For example: Do you endeavour to expand your charm, fairness and balance

14

like someone with Jupiter in Libra, or are you extremely concerned with minor details – making mountains out of molehills, and enjoying analytical work, such as the person with Jupiter in Virgo?

SATURN is the planet of learning. It can therefore restrict, limit and burden our lives with serious intent. This planet can often make us depressed or down in the dumps. For example: Do you feel restricted or frustrated in your innate desire to be a gregarious extrovert, or a distinguished celebrity, as would a person with Saturn in Leo, or do you feel at ease in ponderous, grave situations, with ample time to work matters out thoroughly, like somebody with Saturn in Capricorn?

URANUS rules everything that is unusual, or happens suddenly in our lives. It can disrupt, be extremely unconventional and rebellious, yet also exciting. For example: Are you a live-wire who is stimulated by change, variety, knowledge and learning, which is indicative of Uranus placed in Gemini, or do you feel threatened by life's ups and downs, yet often find that you are forced by circumstances to change your environment, jobs, attitudes, etc., as could happen with Uranus placed in Taurus?

NEPTUNE is the planet of mystery. It rules escapism, confusion, spirituality. It is nebulous and difficult to understand, being indicative of the subconscious on a very deep level. It can cast us down to evil depths, or elevate us into the highest elements of love and creativity. For example: Do you sometimes feel as if you are not truly of this world – that there is something or somebody out there ruling your life, directing you into good or evil, as might be the experience of a person with Neptune in Pisces, or are you a highly practical person, who for no logical reason, occasionally becomes confused and irrational about the fundamental, materialistic side of life, as could happen with Neptune placed in the sign of Capricorn?

PLUTO is a tiny, but powerful planet. It tends to rule behind the scenes and invariably comes out on top. It is significant of eruptions, transformations, birth, death and rebirth. For example: Were you born in the 1940s or 1950s during the generation of people born with Pluto situated in the sign of Leo (indicating that your personal ego and individuality would be dogged throughout your life by major upheavals and the need for transformation)? Or, were you born in the 1960s when the mighty power of Pluto moving through the mundane, critical sign of Virgo, created a generation of highly strung, restless individuals continually striving to cope with the stress caused by the intensity of eruptive Pluto in such a practical, reserved sign?

SIGN GROUPINGS AND INTERPRETATIONS

T he signs of the zodiac can be divided into three major interpretive groups, all of which are extremely important in summarizing an individual's character. This chapter will teach you how to classify a person into the broad categories of extrovert or introvert, dependable or changeable, etc.

ACTIVE AND PASSIVE

The 12 signs are divided into 2 groups of 6, which are labelled Active/Passive (or Masculine/Feminine, or Positive/Negative). Having already learnt the sequence of the signs of the zodiac it is easy to apportion each sign to its appropriate heading. Starting with the sign of Aries, which is active, every alternate and odd-numbered sign, ending with the 11th sign of Aquarius, is also active. Commencing with the second sign of Taurus, which is passive, each alternate and even-numbered sign, ending with the 12th sign of Pisces, is also passive.

Active Signs
Aries, Libra,
Gemini, Sagittarius
Leo, Aquarius

Passive Signs
Taurus, Scorpio
Cancer, Capricorn
Virgo, Pisces

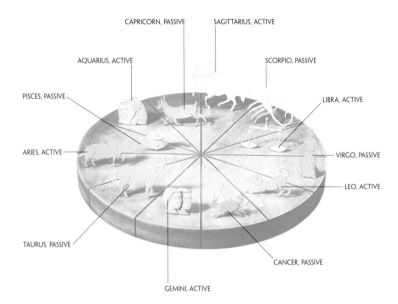

CAPRICORN, PASSIVE
SAGITTARIUS, ACTIVE
AQUARIUS, ACTIVE
SCORPIO, PASSIVE
PISCES, PASSIVE
LIBRA, ACTIVE
ARIES, ACTIVE
VIRGO, PASSIVE
LEO, ACTIVE
TAURUS, PASSIVE
CANCER, PASSIVE
GEMINI, ACTIVE

18

ABOVE WORKING AROUND THE ZODIAC, THE SIGNS, STARTING WITH ARIES AND ENDING WITH AQUARIUS, ALTERNATE BETWEEN ACTIVE AND PASSIVE.

Active signs tend to react forcefully, energetically, positively, unthinkingly. Typically, they are the feet first, head later, individuals who are relatively confident of their position in life. They lack introspectiveness, and are considered to be the extroverts of the zodiac. Passive signs are more contemplative. They can be retiring, unforthcoming and reticent. They are rarely impulsive, or showy, and often prefer to work quietly behind the scenes, but because they think before they act, they often come up trumps, eventually succeeding where the Active person can fail. They

LEFT THE ACTIVE SIGNS ARE CONSIDERED TO BE THE EXTROVERTS OF THE ZODIAC.

THE FOUR ELEMENTS

In this extremely important division of the zodiac, four groups of the signs are allocated a certain element, Fire, Earth, Air or Water:

FIRE	EARTH	AIR	WATER
Aries	Taurus	Gemini	Cancer
Leo	Virgo	Libra	Scorpio
Sagittarius	Capricorn	Aquarius	Pisces

are the introverts of the zodiac. The majority of people, however, are a blend of Active and Passive, with one factor slightly dominant, and it is very rare to find an individual with all ten planets situated in one specific group.

You will note from the above that all the Fire and Air signs are Active and all the Earth and Water are Passive. Each of the four elements possesses favourable, positive characteristics and detrimental negative characteristics, as listed below.

FIRE

These signs can be ardent, enthusiastic, energetic, warm, outgoing, forthright, honest, uncomplicated, optimistic, adventurous, magnetic,

or aggressive, domineering, blunt, offensive, impatient, egotistical, chauvinistic, thoughtless, itinerant, hot-tempered.

EARTH

This element can produce people who are steady, reliable, practical, down-to-earth, businesslike, loyal, sensible, upright, hardworking, patient, analytical, precise,

or dull, materialistic, ruthless, critical, lascivious, mean, slovenly, over-serious, stubborn, self-righteous, depressive.

AIR

People born with many planets in this element are usually communicative, lively, intellectual, resourceful, inventive, calm, logical, charming, sociable, talented,

or self-opinionated, detached, cold, haughty, impractical, eccentric, highly strung, lacking in direction, unfeeling.

WATER

Individuals with this element strong in their chart can be sensitive, kind, protective, artistic, caring, sacrificial, sympathetic, supportive, intuitive, easy-going, spiritual,

or grasping, over-emotional, controlling, addictive, lacking in standards or morals, untidy, dreamy, destructive, revengeful.

QUADRUPLICITIES

The signs can be further divided into three groups of four:

Cardinal	*Fixed*	*Mutable*
Aries, Fire	Taurus, Earth	Gemini, Air
Cancer, Water	Leo, Fire	Virgo, Earth
Libra, Air	Scorpio, Water	Sagittarius, Fire
Capricorn, Earth	Aquarius, Air	Pisces, Water

You will notice that all three groups are formed by taking one sign from each of the four elements. Contrary and diverse as this may seem, all of the four signs in each group possess a certain similarity of character described below:

CARDINAL

Cardinal signs seek out what they want in life, pushing themselves to the forefront of activity, making sure that their voices are somehow heard in the crowd. They are regarded as the self-starters, the initiators of the zodiac and can often appear self-centred. Each sign within this group, however, tends to push itself in a different manner.

Aries (cardinal fire) pushes with brashness and physical force. Lacking in finesse, a strongly Aries person will think nothing of bullying their way to the front of the queue or leading a group of people with brave, reckless abandon. Ariens will always make themselves conspicuous in the most direct manner possible but they can be daring, exciting people with a love of adventure.

Cancer (cardinal water) pushes with slow, sideways movements. They are far too easily hurt to consider aiming directly for their objectives, so they move in a seemingly indifferent, roundabout manner, only pouncing when they are sure of acceptance. They will also endeavour to achieve their own ends by appealing to the emotions of others – probing their way slowly and deftly into the centre of your heart, with their kindly, nurturing ways.

Libra (cardinal air) pushes with such polite consideration and charm that only the most discerning of people will realize that the true aim of this cool sign is in the furthering of their own needs and desires. Diplomacy, tact and finesse are used in abundance by clever, unobtrusive Librans and in no time at all they achieve their purpose as others willingly lend a helping hand. They are usually respected for their harmonious dispositions.

Capricorn (cardinal earth) pushes with cautious, plodding, insidious deliberation. Basically passive and shy like the Cancerian, they find it difficult to move to the front with speed. They know what they want and are determined to achieve their aims, but often have to wait for an eternity before mustering the courage and confidence to make the most of their opportunities. Occasionally they can become ruthless in their objectives, using or abusing others in order to attain their goal. But patience is a word they truly understand.

FIXED

Fixed signs live up to their name. They can be tremendously set in their ways and stubborn to the point of stupidity. Too much of this grouping in a birth chart can cause self-induced ruts, lack of direction in life, and a problem in adjusting to changing circumstances. On the other hand they are loyal, tenacious, dedicated and highly capable, with a remarkably good business acumen and executive streak. When strongly fixed individuals decide that another person is worthy of their esteem, they can also be remarkably generous, and supportive. Adamant, egocentric and unchanging, however, they often suffer more than the other groupings when trauma or difficulties occur in their lives. All the fixed signs will hang on with grim determination to everything they value in life.

Taurus (fixed earth) This sign is the most accumulative in materialistic issues. Financial status and worldly possessions represent security to the stolid but passive Taurean. You will therefore rarely find an extremely poor individual born under this sign – their persistent, tenacious natures stand them in good stead. Once these people decide upon a course of action (often after extreme deliberation) nothing on earth will deter them. Fixed earth is exactly as it sounds – strong and unyielding even under a muddy surface.

Leo (fixed fire) Leo's flames burn steadily and brightly. This sign too is unyielding but not so much with possessions and belongings as with their own resources, their egos and their creativity. If this sign decides to rear itself up from its lazy behind (think of the male lion sleeping all day!) then the heights they can achieve through sheer strength of character, determination and talent are remarkable. However, they do expect a just reward for their painstaking efforts – and nothing suits this vain, but likeable sign, better than being worshipped and idolized by their multitude of followers. Financial remuneration falls a poor second to their love of being loved! It is extremely difficult to put out a Leo fire once it has been started.

Scorpio (fixed water) The still, deep waters of huge lakes describe very aptly the qualities of this intensely emotional fixed sign. Scorpio people will hang on to their feelings – love, jealousy, hate, power, possessiveness, until the bitter end. The problem is that the deep water of these beautiful lakes cannot go anywhere. It remains still and stagnant underneath, unlike the swirling oceans of Cancer and the flowing rivers of Pisces. Scorpio emotions, therefore, are usually held in check. They possess all the tenacity, and determination of the other fixed signs, but it is their feelings and emotions which are the crucial point of their extreme perseverance.

Aquarius (fixed air) Strongly opinionated, utterly assured that they are correct, Aquarian people will always endeavour to convince others of the errors of their ways. This is the sign of fixed mental attitudes. Aquarians possess clever minds, friendly, sociable demeanours and unrivalled talent, but all too often they are overbearing in their dogmatic views. A strongly Aquarian individual will rarely see the other side of the coin, and this invariably leads to his downfall. In no time at all, however, these unusual individuals will be pursuing yet another theme, humanitarian cause or creative talent to grace the world.

23

MUTABLE

Mutable signs are essentially adaptable. They lack the drive of the cardinal signs and the dedication of the fixed signs, but they do possess an innate ability to change their way of life, if necessary. All too often, however, they are pulled in varying

RIGHT THE STRONGLY OPINIONATED AQUARIAN WILL OFTEN
TRY TO CONVINCE OTHERS THAT HE OR SHE IS RIGHT.

directions by stronger individuals than themselves. Generally speaking, these signs have speedy minds and learn easily, but they can forget and lose interest quickly if not stimulated enough. They are the extreme antithesis of the fixed sign quadruplicity. All four mutable signs project their somewhat dissipated energy in a different manner, however.

Gemini (mutable air) Lively, versatile, extremely intelligent and quick-witted, Geminians have a tendency to scatter their mental ability too much. They love learning or attempting to do anything that taxes their enquiring minds. They are interesting people who can talk their way into, or out of, any given situation, but they seldom stay around long enough to reap any long-standing rewards. Loyalty is definitely not their forte, so don't expect them to be around when you need them.

Virgo (mutable earth) Shifting, moving earth, is uncommon – only occasionally rearing its head in the form of earthquakes or other strange phenomena. It therefore stands to reason that Virgo is an extremely difficult sign to understand. They are restless in practical, down-to-earth, mundane matters and can become critical and resentful when communication or movement is restricted. If pressurized too much they can surprise us with their tumultuous energy and ability to destroy. The subjects of this Mercury-ruled sign tend to use their mental attributes in a more practical way than Geminians.

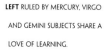

LEFT RULED BY MERCURY, VIRGO AND GEMINI SUBJECTS SHARE A LOVE OF LEARNING.

Sagittarius (mutable fire) The enthusiastic energy of this forthright sign continually changes direction. The fire of Sagittarius is swept this way and that, rarely stopping long enough to enable any form of concentrated energy to build up. More dynamic than the cool air sign of Gemini, Sagittarian people can fascinate us with their charm, wit, and outgoing manner. Their biggest problem is that they tend to exaggerate (remember the huge planet Jupiter rules this sign) – and almost anything can be blown up out of proportion. Do not rely upon them too heavily, therefore, to fulfil their promises. They truly mean what they say – when they say it, but come tomorrow all will be forgotten, as their flame of restless, changeable energy burns in a different direction.

Pisces (mutable water) This sign is renowned for its moody sensitivity. Changeable, flowing emotions, like a meandering river, aptly describes the Piscean's feelings. They can feel very strongly about something or someone one day, then be totally averse to the object of their passion the following day. Never expect a Piscean to be constant. It is this very inconstancy that leads this sign to seek out all forms of escapism. But just as the river eventually flows out into the sea, the Piscean is capable of putting everything behind him and starting afresh. They learn through their feelings and intuition rather than by accepted standards.

BIRTH CHART CALCULATION

CHAPTER THREE

As mentioned in the foreword, the calculation of a birth chart can often deter many would-be students from learning astrology. But you don't have to be a mathematical genius to learn how to erect a chart and derive pleasure from the process. Nowadays computers and much pre-printed information, the erection of a birth chart is a great deal easier than it was several hundred years ago.

YOU WILL NEED

PLANETARY EPHEMERIDES

These books list the daily positions of the planets. The most commonly available are as follows:

- *The Concise Planetary Ephemeris for the Years 1900 to 2000* (Noon Edition), available in paperback in two 50-year sections.

ABOVE TO CONSTRUCT A CHART, YOU'LL NEED AN ATLAS, EPHEMERIS AND CALCULATOR.

• *The American Ephemeris for the Years 1900 to 2000 and 2000 to 2050* (Noon Edition), available in one paperback edition.

• *Raphael's Astronomical Ephemeris* for the planets' places for each separate year.

Ideally, you should purchase either of the two complete editions mentioned above ensuring that you acquire a Noon position edition rather than a Midnight edition as all the calculation in this book is based upon the position of the planets at noon. (There is a list of publishers and stockists in Useful Addresses.)

RAPHAEL'S TABLES OF HOUSES

Three small, inexpensive booklets commonly used in birth chart erection:

Tables of Houses for Great Britain

Tables of Houses for Northern Latitudes   Used solely for births

Tables of Houses for Southern Latitudes   outside Great Britain

You'll need to know the time difference from Greenwich Mean Time for the time zone in which your subject was born.

ATLAS OR GAZETTEER

Either of the above would be suitable providing it lists the latitudes and longitudes of all the major towns in the world. It is relatively easy, however, to calculate longitude and latitude positions from maps. Also most computer programs for erecting a birth chart will automatically provide the latitudes and longitudes of major towns in the world.

BIRTH CHART FORMS

These are available from the stockists as listed in Useful Addresses.

Example Calculations

Having spoken about the necessary tools we are now ready to commence with the calculation. For this we will use several fictitious examples increasing in complexity of calculation, as follows:

EXAMPLE 1

(involving minimum calculation)

Female: Born 22 February 1982, at 9.15am, Lewisham, London, UK. Take a blank sheet of paper (or a birth chart form if available) and write on it the above details. The time of birth is extremely important – if you do not know the time of birth (within half-an-hour) then it is extremely difficult to erect a true blueprint of the character at birth.

Time Calculation

You must ensure that the time given is actual Greenwich Mean Time (the whole system of astrological calculation anywhere in the world is based upon converting Greenwich Mean Time to Sidereal Time which is the true or real time derived from the orbits of the planets). As the birth took place in the UK, we must check whether it occurred during British Summertime. If so, then we must deduct one hour from the birth time in order to arrive at Greenwich Mean Time. Certain years during the war adopted Double Summertime, necessitating a deduction of two hours from February 1968 to the end of October 1971. British Standard Time was in operation – the clocks remaining one hour ahead of Greenwich Mean Time throughout the year, so that all births during these years require one hour to be deducted from their birth time. Appendix 1 lists the changing Summertimes from the year 1916 to the present day. Our example female was born during winter hours and therefore her birth time of 9.15am is actual Greenwich Mean Time.

We can now proceed onto the longitude and latitude, but as the birth occurred extremely close to Greenwich no calculation is necessary. (Many London births contain only minimal degrees of longitude due to their close proximity to Greenwich, thereby necessitating very little geographical adjustment.) Towns in the Outer London boroughs, such as Surrey, Middlesex, Essex, etc., should always be included in the longitude, latitude adjustment.

Now, turn to the copy of the relevant page from Raphael's Astronomical Ephemeris for the year 1982 (*See* p.120). You will note that in the column adjacent to 22 February (on the right-hand side) there is another column, marked Sidereal Time. This is the true astronomical time at noon, and is listed as 22 hours, 8 minutes and 15 seconds. The next step is to ascertain the sidereal time for the actual time of birth. (For a person lucky enough to have been born at midday, the following calculation is not necessary.) Depending upon whether the birth occurred during the morning or the afternoon you will need either to subtract or to add to the given sidereal time at noon. Our example was born at 9.15am, thus indicating that we should subtract from the time as follows:

H	M	S
22	08	15
-2	45	00
—	—	—
19	23	15

(Remember that 9.15am is actually 2 hours 45 minutes before noon, but a birth occurring at 9.15pm would necessitate an addition of 9 hours, 15 minutes to the sidereal time. For those of you whose mathematics are a little rusty, do not forget that we are dealing with time: 60 seconds to the minute, 60 minutes to the hour, and 24 hours in a day.)

ACCELERATION

We now have a new sidereal time, but one more slight adjustment is required before we can say this is the actual sidereal time at birth. This is called the acceleration on the interval, and is necessary because sidereal time is actually fractionally faster than Greenwich Mean Time – a sidereal day is completed almost four minutes faster than a Mean Time day. The calculation for this adjustment is extremely easy, however, and if accidentally omitted from a birth chart it will not radically alter the final result.

To calculate the acceleration on the interval you must allow ten seconds for every hour of difference in time, before or from noon. Our example has a difference of 2 hours 45 minutes, giving an acceleration figure of 27 seconds to be deducted from the above worked out sidereal time:

H	M	S	
19	23	15	- Acceleration on interval 27
		27	(10 sec per hour)
—	—	—	
19	22	48	

Remember always to put this figure in the seconds column (or minutes and seconds if the result is above 60 seconds). The maximum amount of acceleration in any calculation is only two minutes – an extremely small amount, but it would drastically alter the chart if it were placed in the wrong column(s)!

Having arrived at the new sidereal time of 19 22 48 we should now look at the longitude figure. In this first example, however, there is no longitude to calculate as the child was born close to Greenwich. No other adjustments being required, we have therefore reached the sidereal time for this child at her time of birth.

CALCULATING THE ASCENDANT

From this figure we are able to find out the Ascendant, (Rising Sign – *See* chapter 7) which rules the personality structure of the child, and erect the personal birth chart.

Turn to the copy of the *Table of Houses for London* (Latitude 51 degrees 32 minutes North) on page 22, and look down the column marked Sidereal Time until you find the nearest figure to our time of 19 22 48, which is 19 22 18. Look across (to the right) to the column marked 'Ascen' and you will find the figure of 14 degrees, 35 minutes. Glancing upwards you will find the glyph (symbol) for the sign of Taurus situated half way down the column. This is the Ascending sign. Glancing across to the left under the column marked 10 (next to the Sidereal Time section) you will see the figure 19 which means 19 degrees. Glancing upwards, underneath the number 10 there is the symbol for the sign of Capricorn. This sign is the Midheaven – the highest point in the birth chart – an extremely important part of astrology, the meaning of which will be explained in chapter 8.

We have so far thus calculated that our Example's Ascendant is 14 degrees 35 minutes in the sign of Taurus, with her Midheaven at 19 degrees in the sign of Capricorn. From this information we are able to erect the birth chart as detailed in chapter 4. Before we move on to this chapter, however, it is important that you grasp the principles of calculation and for that several more examples of a slightly more complex nature are required.

EXAMPLE 2

(a more involved example, using Summertime and Longitude)
Male, born 6 July 1941 at 11.40pm in Liverpool, England.

Using the same procedure as in the previous example, write down the above details on plain paper or a chart form. The birth time as given, is 11.40pm, but upon checking our Summertime list in Appendix 1, we find that during World War Two, Double Summertime was in operation from 4 May to 10 August, thereby necessitating a deduction of two hours to make the time of birth 9.40 pm Greenwich Mean Time.

SIDEREAL TIME

Turn to the reproduction of *Raphael's Astronomical Ephemeris* for the year 1941 on pages 116–117, and for the date 6 July you will note that the sidereal time at noon is 6 56 18. Because our subject's birth occurred in the afternoon, we need to add on the difference from noon, thus:

H	M	S
6	56	18
+9	40	00
—	—	—
16	36	18

ACCELERATION

Now we deal with the acceleration on the interval, which is also added on due to the pm birth. remember to allow 10 seconds per hour, which means 5 seconds per half-hour, 2–3 for every quarter of an hour.) In this case, 9 hours 40 minutes difference results in an acceleration of approximately 97 seconds = 1 minute 37 seconds:

16	36	18
+	01	37
—	—	—
16	37	55

Because our subject was born in Liverpool we need to work out a slight longitude adjustment. After checking in our atlas/gazetteer we find that the longitude for Liverpool is 2 degrees 58 minutes West. We should write this figure in the appropriate section on the chart form or after the date and time of birth on a sheet of paper.

To calculate the longitude equivalent we must multiply the longitude figure by four, the result, depending upon the size of the longitude, being in hours, minutes and seconds. A small longitude as in the case of Liverpool is relatively easy to work out:

2 degrees 58 minutes X 4 = 11 minutes 52 seconds.

This figure must now be added or subtracted from the calculated sidereal time. If the longitude is east of Greenwich you must add the resulting figure – if it is west of Greenwich you must subtract the figure. Liverpool is west of Greenwich so we must subtract the resulting 11 minutes 52 seconds:

H	M	S
16	37	55
-	11	52
—	—	—
16	26	03

This is the final adjustment and therefore the true sidereal time at birth of the subject of our example.

CALCULATING THE ASCENDANT

We must now check through the Table of Houses for Liverpool (Latitude 53 degrees 25 minutes North) as reproduced on page 123 to find the nearest sidereal time. You will notice beneath the 'Ascen' column that 16 26 03 falls midway between the sidereal times of 16 24 55 and 16 29 10:

> 16 24 55 = 6 degrees 58 minutes   Aquarius rising
>
> 16 29 10 = 8 degrees 46 minutes   Aquarius rising

Logically therefore, as our calculated time falls midway between the two, so must the Ascendant – giving us a figure of 7 degrees 54 minutes. (If you find this difficult or confusing, then use a calculator.) We need not worry about the minutes involved in this sum – the 7 degrees is more than enough to base a good interpretation.

So we have arrived at an Ascendant of 7 degrees Aquarius for our male subject. Looking across to find the Midheaven degree we find it falls midway between 8 and 9 degrees of Sagittarius, thereby giving us a figure of 8 and a half degrees (8 degrees 30 minutes), but the figure of 8 degrees will suffice.

In chapter 4 we will erect our subject's birth chart using the following calculations:

> Ascendant 7 degrees Aquarius
> Midheaven 8 degrees Sagittarius

EXAMPLE 3

(a birth in the Northern Hemisphere)

Male: Born 2 October 1963 at 9.23pm in New York.

All countries other than Great Britain use their own zone standard time, which must be converted into Greenwich meantime. Some atlases and gazetteers may show zone time-differences, or you may be able to find out the information from your local library, from an airport, or from the appropriate embassy. Margaret Hone's *Modern Textbook of Astrology* contains a fairly comprehensive list of overseas countries' Standard Times.

SIDEREAL TIME

New York, like the UK, keeps Summertime. (Many countries do not keep Summertime, and therefore require no adjustment.) We must therefore add five hours onto the time of birth, giving us a time of 2.23am 3 October 1963 (notice we have moved on a day in this country). The one hour Summertime must now be deducted to arrive at the time of 1.23am Greenwich Mean Time. All our calculation from now on is based on the time 1.23am 3 October 1963.

The sidereal time at noon on this day (check with the copy of *Raphael's Astronomical Ephemeris* for October 1963) shown on pages 116–121, is 12 45 53. From this time we need to deduct the amount of interval, which is 10 hours 37 minutes to noon:

H	M	S
12	45	53
-10	37	00
—	—	—
02	08	53

ACCELERATION

We now also deduct the acceleration on the interval, which amounts to 109 seconds = 1 minute 49 seconds

02	08	53
-	01	49
—	—	—
02	07	04

Then we move on to the longitude conversion. New York is 74 degrees West of Greenwich which, converted to time = 4 hours 56 minutes. This difference must now be subtracted from the above sidereal time:

H	M	S
02	07	04
-04	56	00
—	—	—
21	11	04

You will note from the above calculation that 24 hours has been added on to the initial 2 hours of sidereal time in order to subtract the 4 hours 56 minutes.

CALCULATING THE ASCENDENT

We have now arrived at the actual sidereal time at birth for our American subject, and can turn to the appropriate Tables of Houses – those for New York (latitude 40 degrees 40 minutes North), shown on page 124. The sidereal time of 21 11 04 is midway between 21 09 53 and 21 13 52. The Ascendant should therefore fall midway between the two figures of 9 degrees 23 minutes of the sign Gemini and 10 degrees 28 minutes of Gemini, which produces a figure of approximately 9 degrees 56 minutes. A rounded-up figure of 10 degrees of Gemini will be sufficient for the Ascending degree. Glancing left to the column marked 10, we find 15 degrees of Aquarius on the Midheaven.

Our American example therefore possesses:

Ascendant 10 degrees Gemini
Midheaven 15 degrees Aquarius

SOUTHERN HEMISPHERE CALCULATIONS

For a birth occurring in the Southern Hemisphere (for example, Australia), the same formula is followed as for a Northern Hemisphere birth until the local (final) sidereal time is reached, whereupon a further 12 hours must be added on. The Table of Houses for Southern Latitudes is then required in order to find the Ascendant

35

and Midheaven. Once these have been found, the two signs are reversed to arrive at the final result. For instance, if the Ascendant were found to be 11 degrees Libra and the Midheaven 15 degrees Cancer, the reversal would make 11 degrees of Aries the Ascendant, and is degrees of Capricorn the Midheaven.

TIPS FOR CALCULATING THE ASCENDANT AND MIDHEAVEN

Here are some important points to remember when calculating the Ascendant and Midheaven positions in a birth chart.

1 Always write the full details down, preferably on a birth chart form.

2 Remember to use the appropriate Table of Houses for the nearest equivalent latitude.

3 When the local sidereal time amounts to more than 24 hours, always subtract 24 hours. Likewise, if need be, when the hours column is too large to be deducted from the other, always add 24 hours on to the sum you are subtracting from.

4 A birth occuring in the very early hours of the morning in Great Britain can sometimes go back to the preceding day if there are one or two hours of Summertime to be deducted. Always calculate the birth chart from the actual Greenwich Mean Time arrived at after the deduction of Summertime.

5 Acceleration on the interval is 10 seconds per hour and can only be a maximum of 2 minutes in any given day. Do not make the mistake of placing this in the hours column.

6 The longitude figure is always multiplied by four, the answer being in hours, minutes and seconds. East of Greenwich longitudes are always added on, whilst West of Greenwich longitudes are always subtracted.

CONSTRUCTING A BIRTH CHART

I n this chapter we are going to erect the three birth charts calculated in chapter 3. This process is much easier if you have a blank chart form.

EXAMPLE 1

Female: Born 22 February 1982 at 9.15am, Lewisham, London, UK. Ascendant 14 degrees Taurus, Midheaven 19 degrees Capricorn.

Using a blank chart form (or drawing your own circle of 360 degrees) the first task is to place the calculated Ascendant into the correct position, which is always on the left-hand side of the circle (*see* diagram 1, page 38).

THE ASCENDANT

Counting each dividing outer ring segment as 0 degrees, count down (in an anti-clockwise direction) to 14 degrees and place a short line or dot at this position. You will notice that each of the 12 segments is divided into 30 degrees (the number of degrees for each sign of the zodiac) and further divided into 5 degree sections. Place another dot or line at the next 14 degree section and the next, until you have placed 12 marks in the circle, as in diagram 1. A word of advice here, if the Ascendant is calculated between 0 and 15 degrees (of any sign)

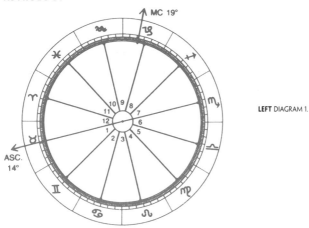

LEFT DIAGRAM 1.

then it is better to count down from the central left 0 degree segment
as in our example, but if the Ascendant is calculated to be between
16 and 29 degrees of a sign, then it is neater and more readable to
place the degree of Ascendant by counting upwards in clockwise
direction from the central segment divider.

It is now necessary to draw 12 equal segments from the 14 degree
position and mark in pencil the Ascendant and its degree as shown
in Diagram 2, either by means of an arrow or different colour. Then
beginning with the segment immediately under the 14 degree
Ascendant, write in (close to the small central circle) the numbers 1
to 12 as shown in diagram 1. These 12 segments are called houses
and are an extremely important part of chart interpretation as
explained in chapter 7.

THE MIDHEAVEN

Now, moving in an anti-clockwise direction again, in the outer circle
write in the signs of the zodiac, commencing with the sign Taurus, by
the arrowed Ascendant, moving in sequence through Gemini, Cancer,
Leo, and so on, always remembering to write in symbols. Having
done this, we should then enter in the Midheaven, at 19 degrees of
Capricorn, with a short arrow (check with diagram 1). With the
system of house division which we are learning, Equal House, the

Midheaven must fall in either the 8th, 9th, 10th or 11th house, the ninth and tenth being the most commonly found. if you arrive at any other position, then you have made an error somewhere and should check your calculations.

THE PLANETS

We are now ready to place in the circle the ten planets described in chapter 1.

Turn to page 120–121, where our copy of *Raphael's Ephemeris* for the month of February 1982 is shown, and find on your immediate left-hand side Monday 22 February. The second column along from this date shows us the position of the Sun at noon, which is 3 degrees 32 minutes in the sign of Pisces (note the change from Aquarius to Pisces on 19 February). As the Sun moves one degree per day, and therefore 30 minutes every 12 hours (half a day), 15 minutes every 6 hours, and 7 and a half minutes every 3 hours, we now have to ascertain whether our subject, born at 9.15am, 2 and three-quarters hours before midday, still has the Sun situated at 3 degrees of Pisces. The time differential in this instance shows that the Sun is situated at approximately 6 minutes less than 3 degrees 32 minutes – that is, at 3 degrees 26 minutes. Three degrees of Pisces then is the position of the Sun in our example's chart. Find this position on your chart form and write in the symbol for the Sun, with the relevant degrees as shown in diagram 2 on page 41.

Next, we place the Moon into position on the chart form, using a similar procedure. Move across to the fourth column on the February 1982 ephemeris, marked Long. at the top, where you will see that the position of the Moon at noon on this day is 17 degrees 3 minutes Aquarius. The Moon is the swiftest-moving planet, completing its cycle in 28 days, and therefore 1 sign (one-twelfth) of the zodiac in approximately 2 and a half days. Using this calculation we can deduce that the Moon moves approximately one degree every two hours. This formula is very important to remember, as unless a person is born at noon, the degrees of the Moon according to the time of birth, are going to be slightly different to those stated in the ephemeris. The calculation is minimal and easy to work out in your head, but you can always use a calculator if necessary. Our subject, therefore, born at 9.15am, two and three quarter hours before noon, should have a Moon movement of almost 1 and a half degrees (around 1 degree 27 minutes). Deduct this figure from 17 degrees 3 minutes and you arrive at 15 degrees 36 minutes. We need not concern ourselves with the minutes at this stage as they are not pertinent to the general interpretation of a birth chart, and can now place the Moon in the birth chart at 15 degrees of Aquarius (*see* diagram 2). Do remember, as with the calculation of the Ascendant that for any time after noon, addition will need to be used, and for any time before noon, subtraction.

Moving across to the right-hand side of our ephemeris page, ignoring all the remaining figures for the Moon, we arrive at the position of the planet Mercury at noon: 7 degrees 3 minutes of the sign Aquarius. You may notice at this stage, further up this column the letter D, which is short for Direct and the symbol ℞ which means Retrograde. When a planet is listed as retrograde it appears from Earth to be moving in a backward motion. Once it begins to move forward again the Direct symbol is used as an indication. The interpretation of a retrograde planet is shown in chapter 8. The retrograde symbol should always be entered into the birth chart, if applicable. (Note in diagram 2 that the planets Mars, Saturn and Pluto are all in retrograde position.) The planet Mercury moves at a variable speed, sometimes moving only a few minutes per day and at others moving as much as 2 degrees per day. Its speed of motion can easily be ascertained by glancing at the previous day's position and then at the following day. On 22 February 1982, we can see that Mercury is not even moving 1 degree a day. From noon on 21 February to noon on the 22nd it has moved only 47 minutes. As you can see, however, at noon on the 22nd it has only just reached 7 degrees and 3 minutes. On the assumption of the planet moving 47 minutes over 24 hours, it will move approximately 6 minutes over 3 hours (a calculator may be required here), and therefore, the 2 and 3 quarter hour time-difference will necessitate around 5 to 6 minutes being deducted from the noon figures, thereby making the position of Mercury at 9.15am to be approximately 6 degrees 58 minutes. Mercury should therefore be written in the chart form as 6 degrees Aquarius as in diagram 2. It would not matter greatly, however, if 7 degrees were written in, as the final figure is so close.

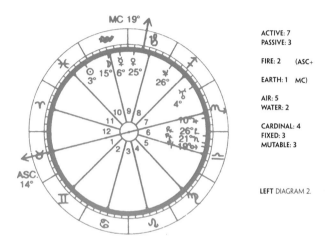

ACTIVE: 7
PASSIVE: 3

FIRE: 2   (ASC+

EARTH: 1   MC)

AIR: 5
WATER: 2

CARDINAL: 4
FIXED: 3
MUTABLE: 3

LEFT DIAGRAM 2.

Now on to Venus – another planet which moves at a variable speed, but rarely as fast as Mercury when at its speediest. From our ephemeris page we can see that Venus is moving particularly slowly during February. (Usually it will travel through a whole sign in less than 30 days.) As it stands at 25 degrees of Capricorn on the 21st and still at 25 degrees of this sign on the 22nd, we can safely write in Venus at this position as in diagram 2.

Mars can spend as long as six months in one sign, and only occasionally requires any further calculation from its noon position. On 22 February 1982, Mars is moving extremely slowly and has just gone retrograde (on 21 February). Its position therefore is 19 degrees Libra, as stated in the Ephemeris. Place this in your birth chart form as shown in diagram 2.

The remaining planets are all too slow-moving to make any degree adjustments necessary, and are therefore written on the chart form as listed in the ephemeris: Jupiter at 10 degrees Scorpio; Saturn at 21 Libra, retrograde; Uranus at 4 degrees Sagittarius; Neptune at 26 degrees Sagittarius; and Pluto at 26 degrees Libra, retrograde.

Our birth chart is now complete with Ascendant, Midheaven and all ten planets listed.

The next step is to list on the chart form or on a sheet of paper the division of the planetary positions into Active and Passive, Elements and Quadruplicities. These listings alone will give remarkable insight into the character of the subject. As there are ten planets within the chart, each division must add up to ten. In Example 1, the following applies.

Active/Passive

Active: (positive)	7	(Moon, Mercury, Mars, Saturn, Uranus, Neptune and Pluto)
Passive: (negative)	3	(Sun, Venus and Jupiter)

Elements

Fire	2	(Uranus and Neptune)
Earth	1	(Venus)
Air	5	(Moon, Mercury, Mars, Saturn and Pluto)
Water	2	(Sun and Jupiter)

Then add the Ascendant and Midheaven (Medium Coeli, MC for short) elements to the total. In this instance both are in Earth, extending the Earth element total to three. (Note how this is entered in diagram 2.)

Quadruplicities

Cardinal	4	(Venus, Mars, Saturn and Pluto)
Fixed	3	(Moon, Mercury and Jupiter)
Mutable	3	(Sun, Uranus and Neptune)

EXAMPLE 2

Male: Born 6 July 1941 at 11.40pm (9.40pm GMT) in Liverpool, UK. Ascendant 7 degrees Aquarius. Midheaven 8 degrees Sagittarius. Adopting the same procedure as in Example 1, first mark out each 7 degree section, and then draw up the house lines (these are called cusps and will be referred to as such from now on). Write in the house numbers, the Ascending sign and degree and the remaining signs in order on the chart wheel. Lastly mark in the Midheaven. Next, turn to the relevant extract from *Raphael's Ephemeris* for the year 1941 (*See* p.117) and find the position of the Sun at noon in the second column along from the left marked 'Sun Long', which is 14 degrees of Cancer exactly. As our subject was born at 9.40pm Greenwich Mean Time we would need to add minutes on to this degree, amounting to approximately 24 minutes, thereby making the position of the Sun 14 degrees 24 minutes. Fourteen degrees alone will suffice and should be entered in the birth chart (as shown in diagram 3).

Looking across to the Moon's longitude column (fourth) we find a noon position of 12 degrees 5 minutes Sagittarius, which necessitates the addition (remember this is a pm birth) of several degrees to be correct for the birth time of 9.40pm. Using our formula of 1 degree for every 2 hours we find that 9 hours 40 minutes from noon requires an addition of just under 5 degrees to our noon position of 12 degrees 5 minutes, thereby increasing it to approximately 17 degrees Sagittarius. This should now be entered in the relevant position (shown in diagram 3).

Work across to the far right where the position for the planet Mercury is shown. You will notice that in this and earlier ephemeris editions the positioning of the planets from Mercury to Neptune is from right to left, but most modern editions list left to right. Check your symbols carefully therefore before proceeding. Pluto is not listed in earlier single-year ephemerides. Abbreviated details of Pluto's movements between the years 1900 to 1970 are listed in Appendix 2.

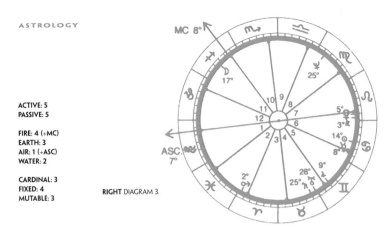

ACTIVE: 5
PASSIVE: 5

FIRE: 4 (+MC)
EARTH: 3
AIR: 1 (+ASC)
WATER: 2

CARDINAL: 3
FIXED: 4
MUTABLE: 3

RIGHT DIAGRAM 3.

The position of Mercury at noon on July is 8 degrees 28 minutes Cancer, retrograde. This means that the planet is moving in a backward motion and will remain at 8 degrees until the following day. Enter Mercury into the chart as shown in diagram 3.

Venus is listed at 4 degrees 52 minutes in the sign of Leo and moving fairly quickly (note it has travelled 1 degree, 13 minutes since the previous day). It is therefore logical to presume that Venus will have reached well over 5 degrees of Leo at the birthtime of 9.40pm, and should be entered into the chart at this degree (diagram 3).

Mars is at 2 degrees 27 minutes of Aries at noon, and not moving fast enough for any adjustment, so enter 2 degrees into the chart. Jupiter is at 9 degrees of Gemini. Saturn is at 24 degrees 58 minutes of Taurus at noon and therefore requires a rare adjustment as it will just reach 25 degrees Taurus by 9.40pm. Uranus is at 28 degrees of Taurus, and Neptune at 25 degrees Virgo. Check Appendix 2 to find Pluto's degree on 6 July 1941 - 3 degrees of Leo, and enter all these positions into the chart, to complete the wheel, as in diagram 3.

Now we can enter the Active/Passive ratio, Elements and Quadruplicities as follows.

Active/Passive

Active	5	(Moon, Venus, Mars, Jupiter and Pluto)
Passive	5	(Sun, Mercury, Saturn, Uranus and Neptune)

Elements

Fire	4(+MC)	(Moon, Venus, Mars and Pluto)
Earth	3	(Saturn, Uranus and Neptune)
Air	1(+ASC)	(Jupiter)
Water	2	(Sun and Mercury)

Quadruplicities

Cardinal	3	(Sun, Mercury and Mars)
Fixed	4	(Venus, Saturn, Uranus and Pluto)
Mutable	3	(Moon, Jupiter and Neptune)

EXAMPLE 3

Male: Born 2 October 1963 at 9.23pm (1.23am GMT 3 October 1963), in New York, USA. Ascendant 10 degrees Gemini, Midheaven 15 degrees Aquarius.

45

Enter in all the relevant information before turning to the planets' positions. Refer to diagram 4 if you feel unsure.

Then enter the planets. Remember, for calculation and planetary adjustment purpose, that we are dealing with a new date and time: 1.23am on 3 October 1963. Try to write in the planets' degrees without any referral.

You should arrive at the following positions:

Sun 9 degrees Libra, Moon 8 degrees Aries, Mercury 21 Virgo, Venus 18 degrees Libra, Mars 14 degrees Scorpio, Jupiter 15 degrees Aries, retrograde, Saturn 16 degrees Aquarius, retrograde, Uranus 7 degrees Virgo, Neptune 14 degrees Scorpio and Pluto 12 degrees Virgo. Count the planets in the three different groupings as usual.

Active/Passive

Active	5	(Sun, Moon, Venus, Jupiter and Saturn)
Passive	5	(Mercury, Mars, Uranus, Neptune and Pluto)

Elements

Fire	2	(Moon and Jupiter)
Earth	3	(Mercury, Uranus and Pluto)
Air	3	(+ ASC and MC) (Sun, Venus and Saturn)
Water	2	(Mars and Neptune)

Quadruplicities

Cardinal	4	(Sun, Moon, Venus and Jupiter)
Fixed	3	(Mars, Saturn and Neptune)
Mutable	3	(Mercury, Uranus and Pluto)

Check the completed chart with diagram 4.

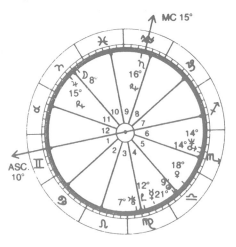

ABOVE DIAGRAM 4.

CALCULATION
OF ASPECTS

CHAPTER FIVE

We are now almost at the end of the calculation stage of a natal birth chart, but before moving on to the interpretation we need to learn about the aspects which the planets make with one another and the important impact these make upon our characters. Because the zodiac wheel consists of 360 degrees divided into 12 sections of 30 degrees, the main aspects used by astrologers are those divisible by 30, of which there are seven.

THE CONJUNCTION

Any two (or more) planets positioned in the chart together, that is, within 8 degrees of one another, are said to be conjunct or in conjunction. The closer the planets, the more important the aspect becomes. For instance, if the planets Mars and Venus were both situated at 20 degrees of Libra, they would be in exact conjunction with one another, but if Mars were at 20 degrees and Venus at either 28 degrees or 12 degrees of Libra they would still be in wide conjunction. The effect of this major aspect can be variable. A conjunction between the two complementary feminine planets Moon and Neptune energizes refinement, delicacy and aesthetic ideals, whereas Moon conjuncting masculine, eccentric Uranus is a turbulent, stress-inducing combination.

Some examples of conjunctions occurring within the three birth charts used in chapters 3 and 4 are:

Example 1 – Mars/Saturn/Pluto
Example 2 – Saturn/Uranus, Mercury/Sun, Pluto, Venus
Example 3 – Uranus/Pluto, Mars/Neptune, Moon/Jupiter.

The conjunction is the easiest of the seven aspects to identify because the planets involved are always extremely close together and usually in the same sign. But be careful, a planet situated at 28 degrees of one sign can still be in conjunction with another at 6 degrees of the following sign.

THE SEMI-SEXTILE ⌄

This is a far less important aspect than the conjunction and involves two (or more) planets situated at a distance of 30 degrees apart. An orb of 2 degrees in either direction is allowable, so, for example, a planet at 10 degrees of Aries would be semi-sextile planets at 12 degrees of Taurus and 8 degrees of Pisces. The effect of this aspect is usually mildly favourable, but once again the temperament of the planets involved must be taken into account.

Some typical examples from our three subjects are:

Example 1 – Neptune-Venus
Example 2 – Jupiter-Mercury
Example 3 – Uranus-Sun

The semi-sextile aspect is relatively easy to identify, as the planets involved are nearly always situated one sign (or house) apart, for example, Aries to Taurus, Taurus to Gemini, Gemini to Cancer, etc., or 1st to 2nd house, 2nd to 3rd house, 3rd to 4th house etc.

THE SEXTILE ✳

The sextile involves two (or more) planets placed 60 degrees apart with an allowable orb of 4 degrees. For example, a planet at 12 degrees of Sagittarius would be sextile planets at 13 degrees of Aquarius and 8 degrees of Libra. The sextile can be one of the most beneficial aspects of all, as the planets involved are usually in signs which are elementally compatible, such as the fire sign Sagittarius with the air signs of Libra and Aquarius, or the earth sign Taurus with the water signs Pisces and Cancer. Air fans the flames of the fire, and earth contains the emotions of the water. For a person with this aspect, therefore, opportunities and optimism, or talents well-utilized are usual.

Some examples from our three subjects:

Example 1 – Pluto-Neptune, Uranus-Mercury
Example 2 – Jupiter-Venus
Example 3 – Pluto/Mars-Neptune, Saturn/Jupiter

Try to recognize the sextile aspect by looking at the signs involved. If they are both active or both passive and the planets 56 to 64 degrees apart (using the 4 degree orb) then they must be forming a sextile.

THE SQUARE ☐

This is one of the major aspects and usually the most potent after the conjunction. It is formed by 2 (or more) planets situated 90 degrees apart, with an allowable 8 degree orb. For example, a planet at 17 degrees of Scorpio will be in square aspect with another at 17 degrees of Leo or another at 10 degrees of Aquarius, the former being an exact square aspect, the latter involving a 7 degree orb.

Invariably a difficult, tension-motivated aspect, the square often causes much trouble within a birth chart, especially during the immature years. A square between two incompatible planets such as Jupiter and Saturn, usually causes more problems than one between two compatible planets such as the Sun and Jupiter. Square aspects can be utilized beneficially, but it takes time, patience and understanding.

Examples of squares in our three subjects' charts are:

Example 1– Mars/Saturn/Pluto-Venus,
                    Jupiter-Mercury, Uranus-Sun
Example 2 – Mars-Mercury, Neptune-Moon
Example 3 – Mars/Neptune-Saturn

Squares are not always easy to identify. If, however, you have learnt the three groupings of the signs thoroughly, you will now be reaping the rewards. All the quadruplicities are in square aspect to one another. For example, planets in Aries may be square to planets in Capricorn or Cancer. Planets in Virgo may be square to any situated in Sagittarius or Gemini. It is possible, however, to have a square between compatible elements – such is the case when one planet is placed very near the end of a sign and another placed near the beginning of a sign, for instance, Moon at 27 degrees of Scorpio would be square Saturn at 3 degrees of Pisces. This type of square would not be quite so difficult.

THE TRINE △

Formed by planets 120 degrees apart and allowing an 8 degree orb, the trine is an aspect which allows ease of operation. It can give great talent or opportunities when motivated. Two usually inharmonious planets, such as Mercury and Saturn will be rendered more accessible to one another through this aspect.

Some examples of trines from our three birth charts:

> Example 1 – Mars/Saturn-Moon, Pluto-Sun (note change of
> element here and 7 degree orb), Jupiter-Sun
>
> Example 2 – Mars-Pluto/Venus, Saturn/Uranus-Neptune
>
> Example 3 – Sun-Saturn, Venus-Saturn

The trine is relatively easy to pick out because it usually occurs between planets situated within the same element. For example, Mars at 8 degrees of Capricorn will be trine to Pluto at 12 degrees of Virgo, and Jupiter at 1 degree of Taurus, the former utilizing a 4 degree orb, the latter a 7 degree orb. However, it is possible for a trine to be formed between incompatible elements. For example, Venus at 29 degrees of Gemini would be in trine to Neptune at 4 degrees of Scorpio. These examples are harmonious, but more invigorating.

THE QUINCUNX/INCONJUNCT ⚻

The very fact that this aspect possesses two different names indicates the complexity of its workings. Planets form a quincunx when they are situated 150 degrees apart with an allowable 2–3 degree orb. The two signs involved in this aspect are nearly always of a different element and Active/Passive grouping. For example, a planet at 14 degrees of Pisces would be quincunx planets at 12 degrees Libra, and 13 degrees Leo. A planet at 2 degrees of Taurus would be quincunx planets at 1 degree of Sagittarius and 3 degrees Libra.

The quincunx is regarded as a minor aspect, somewhat difficult in nature, often related to ill health, stress and adjustments in life. But like the square, when understood and utilized positively, it can give creative potential and diverse talents.

Some examples of quincunxes from our three charts:

Example 1– None

Example 2 – Sun-Moon

Example 3 – Jupiter-Pluto, Moon-Uranus, Neptune/Mars-Jupiter

The quincunx is the hardest of all the aspects for the beginner to see quickly as there is no set grouping of elements or quadruplicities for it to fall within. Time and practice however will give you knowledge as to which signs could provide quincunxes.

THE OPPOSITION ☍

This aspect, as its name suggests involves planets which are immediately opposed to one another – that is, 180 degrees apart. Once again an orb of 8 degrees either way is allowable. The opposition is the most powerful aspect after the conjunction and square, but as it usually involves planets in signs which are compatible, such as Moon at 15 degrees of Sagittarius opposing Sun at 17 degrees of Gemini, it is rarely as problematical as the square or conjunction. One of the effects of this aspect is its see-saw motion. If this is prominent in a chart, the subject will strive to achieve balance and equilibrium in his life and will be prone to polarities of mood.

Some examples of oppositions from the charts of our three subjects:

Example 1 – None

Example 2 – Moon-Jupiter, Mars-Neptune (this widely orbed opposition combines two different elements)

Example 3 – Sun-Moon, Venus-Jupiter

The opposition is easy to determine as the planets involved are opposite one another, and usually posited in complementary elements, such as Fire and Air, or Water and Earth. Watch out for the exceptions, however. Mars at 28 degrees of Taurus would still be in opposition to Pluto at 4 degrees of Sagittarius. This type of opposition could actually be more problematical, as the elements of Earth and Fire do not blend well.

FINDING ASPECTS

The next step is to learn how to recognize the above aspects and place them in the aspect grid on the birth chart form.

The simplest method of finding aspects without any mechanical devices is to learn thoroughly the groupings of the signs as shown in chapter 2 to enable you to be able to recognize instantly which type of aspect planets may be forming. One golden rule to remember is that any two planets beyond an 8 degree orb, such as Mars at 5 degrees of Aries and Jupiter at 15 degrees of Cancer cannot be in aspect. In this case you can instantly see the 10 degree difference signifying that Jupiter is situated precisely 100 degrees from Mars. Conversely, any planets within an 8 degree orb, such as Uranus at 19 degrees Taurus and Venus at 13 degrees Virgo (in this instance, a trine) may be in aspect if they can form a conjunction, square, trine or opposition. Any planets with a 2 degree difference must form some kind of aspect, such as Moon at 18 degrees of Gemini, Mercury at 20 degrees of Capricorn (creating a quincunx).

Many beginners, however, find they cannot easily remember the groupings of the signs and prefer to count the degrees between aspects. This is perfectly acceptable and may provide more accuracy in the first instance. Simply count the degrees between the two planets always remembering to allow the appropriate degrees of orb, if necessary. Diagrams 5 and 6 demonstrate the following examples:

DIAGRAM 5

- Mars at 16 degrees Cancer is 95 degrees away from Jupiter at 21 Libra, thereby forming a square.

ROLOGY

- Neptune at 12 degrees of Scorpio is 58 degrees away from Mercury at 10 degrees of Capricorn, forming a sextile.
- The Sun at 1 degree of Aquarius, is 32 degrees away from Venus at 3 degrees of Pisces, forming a semi-sextile.
- The Moon at 9 degrees of Pisces is 123 degrees from Saturn at 12 degrees of Cancer, thereby forming a trine.

DIAGRAM 6

- Neptune and Saturn are in exact conjunction at 11 degrees of Sagittarius.
- Jupiter at 9 degrees of Aquarius is situated 151 degrees from Venus at 10 degrees of Cancer, forming a quincunx.
- Mars at 22 degrees of Aries is 175 degrees away from Pluto at 17 degrees of Libra (185 degrees apart in the opposite direction), and therefore forms an opposition.

54

To enter aspects on the grid simply work across from left to right starting with the Sun, comparing it with the Moon, then Mercury, then Venus, and so on, finishing with Pluto. Then work across from the Moon, comparing it with Mercury, Venus, Mars, etc. Move on to Mercury, then Venus, etc., until you reach the last two planets to observe for aspects, Neptune and Pluto.

The Ascendant and Midheaven are always used when calculating aspects. Therefore work across in the same manner starting with the Ascendant to Sun, then Moon, etc. Lastly complete the Midheaven section.

If two planets make no aspect to one another it is often clearer and neater to mark the appropriate square with a dot or dash. Diagrams 7–9 show the aspect grids for all three of the examples used in the previous chapters. Study them carefully, ensuring that you understand the mechanics of aspect calculation. Note any unusual patterns, for example, a chart with mainly squares is going to be much more challenging than a chart with mainly trines. Lots of aspects (more than 32) can create a lot of problems.

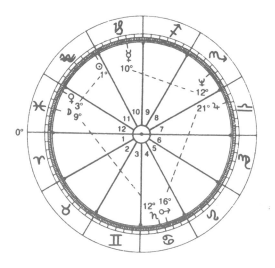

ABOVE DIAGRAM 5.

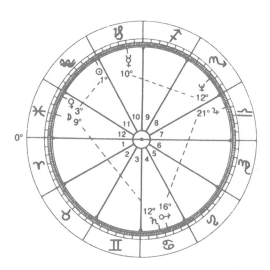

ABOVE DIAGRAM 6.

ABOVE DIAGRAM 7.

ABOVE DIAGRAM 8.

ABOVE DIAGRAM 9.

INTERPRETATION: PLANETS IN SIGNS

CHAPTER SIX

Having completed the calculation of a birth chart it is now time to start interpreting the accumulation of symbols and facts placed before us, a complex task that cannot be achieved overnight – accurate interpretation takes time, study and patience. I would therefore recommend to all students that they are confident in their understanding of the preceding chapters. In this chapter we shall be defining the significance of the 10 planets when situated in the 12 signs of the zodiac. The brief interpretations are in no way conclusive, so try to add your own definitions too.

THE SUN

Rules our ego and individuality, often the deepest, innermost part of our character, which can be hidden from view. We relate to our Sun sign as being our true self, and should strive to achieve the positive characteristics of this sign in order to be living a fulfilled life. Brief keyword definitions for the position of the Sun in all 12 signs are given in chapter 1. Go back and study these interpretations carefully and try to add your own keywords by using the characteristics of the three groupings of the signs and the energy of the ruling planet.

THE MOON

Rules our emotions, feelings, responses and habits. It is extremely important in our birth charts, often overshadowing the Sun, especially in childhood when we have not yet learnt to control our emotions. Many adults who behave irrationally, or immaturely have the Moon strongly placed in their birth chart.

Moon in Aries: An explosive, difficult placement causing sharp, irritable responses. Subject likes own way, is pushy, lacking in finesse, self-centred and childlike in attitude. Loves travelling. Possesses restless, seeking nature which exudes much fiery magnetism.

ABOVE THE MOON RULES OUR EMOTIONS AND IS ESPECIALLY INFLUENTIAL IN CHILDHOOD.

Moon in Taurus: The changeable nature of the Moon is steadied in this sign, giving domesticated, practical, protective, motherly and tenacious qualities. Subject loves land, building and structure and is fastidious with strong materialistic instincts.

Moon in Gemini: Extremely moody, restless and talkative. Fond of expressing emotions in a garrulous manner. Highly intelligent, but often unable to control feelings of duplicity, vengefulness and animosity. Exceptionally witty or overbearingly sarcastic.

Moon in Cancer: Ultra-sensitive, extremely shy and lacking in self-confidence. Strongly attached to mother or mother-figure. Seeks security and steady home-life. Cautious with finances and possessions. Dislikes letting go, possesses strong nurturing instincts.

Moon in Leo: The showman of the zodiac. Will liven up almost any birth chart with its extreme flamboyance and demonstrative reactions. Generous to a fault, loves praise and attention, but can develop tantrums and sulks if feeling unappreciated.

Moon in Virgo: Quiet, serious demeanour, exhibiting cold or unfeeling responses. Feels at ease with detailed, routine work. Health conscious and fastidious about personal hygiene. Inner emotions chaotic and usually repressed.

Moon in Libra: Charming, likeable, attractive, intelligent and outwardly serene, these people will grace any social occasion. At times, they can, however, be remarkably selfish, callous and unfeeling. They enjoy good conversation, harmonious surroundings and affluent company.

Moon in Scorpio: Subject experiences intense, deep feelings. Jealousy, possessiveness or anger simmer beneath a calm façade. Intuitive and probing, they make excellent psychiatrists, detectives or clairvoyants. Mother-dominated as children, they often rebel in adulthood and find it difficult to sustain loving relationships.

Moon in Sagittarius: Changeable and moody, this configuration produces the emotional wanderer of the zodiac, lacking in concentration and loyalty. Possessing a good, but somewhat crude sense of humour, this person can be impractical, buoyant, hysterical and fun loving.

Moon in Capricorn: Repressed, inhibited emotions often caused by severe mothering are common with this placement. The subject strives for security through materialistic means and is capable of using others for his own ends. Steady and persevering, ambitious, and controlled.

Moon in Aquarius: Good, dry sense of humour. Sociable and friendly within a large group, but avoids close relationships. Independent, unusual and creatively talented, but insensitive to the feelings of others. Can, however, become deeply committed to causes, group situations, friends and social outlets.

Moon in Pisces: Dreamy, imaginative, over-sensitive, and often lacking in personal direction. Romantic, poetic, psychic, artistic and creative, they are, however, innately escapist, and dislike the limelight. Changeable in affections, they can be moody, irresponsible, unreliable and prone to excesses in almost anything.

MERCURY

Rules all aspects of communication – the manner in which we learn, listen, speak, write, etc. Being so close to the Sun, it often takes on the characteristics of the Sun sign, but if placed in a different sign it operates totally independently.

Mercury in Aries: Speaks and communicates with speed, enthusiasm, boldness and confidence. Not very good at sustaining attention, or explaining anything in detail. Irritation and short-tempered verbal outbursts are common with this configuration.

Mercury in Taurus: Communication is slow, precise and laboured. Can be dull and boring in speech, but comes to life when singing (a strong Taurean talent). Enjoys communicating on a practical level, either verbally or with hands. Good business sense.

Mercury in Gemini: Situated in the sign of its rulership, Mercury is at its sparkling best. Witty, lively and irrepressible, chatty and excitable, with much surface knowledge, these people are, however, highly strung and can suffer from nervous disorders.

Mercury in Cancer: These people are invariably 'thinkers', rather than 'talkers', often finding it difficult to communicate without expressing emotion. When challenged, however, their verbal reactions can be caustic in their own defence. They possess extremely retentive memories.

Mercury in Leo: Pride, recognition and a need to be heard are qualities commonly expressed by this configuration. Sometimes, however, their propensity for 'all talk and no action' produces exaggeration, boasting or conceit, yet they can be charming, precocious and talented.

Mercury in Virgo: A good, sound mind, capable of great study and learning. Because these people absorb and pass on information quickly and efficiently, they make excellent teachers. Worry and the inability to see the other side of the situation could, however, be their downfall.

Mercury in Libra: This position produces intelligence and speed of learning. Quietly spoken with immense charm, there is always something very pleasant or polite about their demeanour. They may prefer to communicate through writing or music rather than speech.

ABOVE COMMUNICATION THROUGH MUSIC IS OFTEN FOUND IN PEOPLE WITH MERCURY IN LIBRA.

Mercury in Scorpio: A powerful, penetrating mind. Mercury can either be extremely silent and thoughtful here, or verbose. These people never forget, and rarely forgive. Their speech can be harsh or vindictive when angry, but gentle and soothing when in a caring situation.

Mercury in Sagittarius: Extremely communicative, restless and volatile, with a pressing need to talk about anything and everything. These people often give the impression of being more knowledgeable than they really are, and can outwit anybody. They have a hearty sense of humour and love to play pranks or jokes.

Mercury in Capricorn: Quiet, serious manner of expression which can appear taciturn or uncaring. These people find it extremely difficult to communicate, and are often very slow learners. When knowledge is absorbed, however, it is never forgotten, and always put to practical sound use.

Mercury in Aquarius: Produces inventive, ingenious minds, with unusual or erratic manner of communicating. They learn quickly and retain information, but often appear supercilious, and difficult to approach. They are greatly attracted to modern technology as means of communication.

Mercury in Pisces: Tends to communicate on a vague, dreamy level. Brilliant imagination and creative ability, but often unable to structure their capabilities. Will either chat incessantly or remain agonizingly shy and quiet – depending upon whom they are with. These people lack concentration yet are able to absorb knowledge like a sponge.

VENUS

This planet represents love and harmony. It reveals what, who and how we love, and also our values in life. It is not the 'gut' feeling represented by the Moon, but more our mode of appreciation and enjoyment.

Venus in Aries: These people love ardently and fiercely. Quick to show appreciation and quick to tire, they need constant stimulation. They enjoy excitement and danger, and love being in the limelight. They may find it difficult to be loyal or faithful when their sense of adventure is roused.

Venus in Taurus: Placed in a sign of its rulership, Venus is very much at home and can therefore be lazy, complacent and even-tempered. Musical or singing talent is common. These people usually feel in tune with the beauty of nature and like to be in close contact with the land.

Venus in Gemini: Flirtatious, light-hearted and inoffensive, those with Venus in this sign are usually popular, but they can be deceitful or untruthful when confronted with difficult situations. Inconstant, yet delightfully naive, they are easily forgiven. They enjoy talking and communicating on a convivial level.

Venus in Cancer: This sign tends to bring out the best in Venus. These people love with sensitivity, tenderness and compassion. They enjoy entertaining at home, raising a family, photography, films and dealing with antiques. Conscious of the material world, but capable of great acts of charity.

Venus in Leo: Adulation, luxury and adornment, are vitally desired by these people in order that they may project their loving, generous and loyal qualities. If deprived of these requisites they wilt and become sullen and ego-centred. Theatrical involvement is one way in which they can command the respect they crave.

Venus in Virgo: Renowned for their purity and analytical detachment, these complex people often feel misunderstood or underrated. They are extremely fussy, and critical, yet adore animals, small pets especially, whom they turn to for the affection often lacking in their lives.

Venus in Libra: This configuration adds charm, pleasantness and refinement to even the most difficult of birth charts. It can, however, also be conducive to narcissism. Music, dance, art or drama appeals strongly to their aesthetic natures. They believe in justice and harmony, but are rarely very demonstrative when in love.

Venus in Scorpio: Loves deeply, with either much possessiveness, jealousy and insecurity, or with passion, generosity and kindness. They are capable, however, of controlling their feelings of love and withdrawing from society completely. They appreciate mystery, seductiveness, allure, and unhibited sexuality.

ABOVE A LOVE OF SMALL PETS IS OFTEN FOUND IN PEOPLE WITH VENUS IN VIRGO.

Venus in Sagittarius: Amorous and well-intentioned, this person seeks freedom and security in a relationship, a regular once-a-week tryst being regarded as idyllic. They possess a good sense of humour and appreciation of anything large, including animals such as horses, and enjoy active sports.

Venus in Capricorn: Usually quiet, with an appreciation of serious matters, this person is often labelled prudish or frigid, which is far from the truth – they just take longer than most people to warm up. Capable of extreme frugality, they shun luxury and adornment, especially in their youth. They tend to look and act younger than their years.

Venus in Aquarius: Charming and sociable, yet detached and unsympathetic, these subjects enjoy projecting themselves. They are attracted to scientific or electronic gadgets and anything to do with aviation. Often labelled as unfeeling and cold, they will avoid any demonstrations of affection.

Venus in Pisces: Altruistic, soft and loving, yet careless and disorganized, this position produces both saints and sinners. Romantic, sensitive and artistic, they yearn for love and harmony, which all too often alludes them, causing them to become prey to such vices as escapism, decadence or addiction. Self sacrifice is common.

MARS

Physical energy, assertiveness, aggression, sexual and sporting activity and violence all fall under the domain of this highly masculine planet. It toughens and dominates the area of the birth chart in which it is found.

Mars in Aries: Placed within the sign that it rules, Mars is in its prime, endowing its subjects with unlimited energy, a tremendous sense of adventure and a desire to live life to the full. Used negatively it can produce anger, violence, bullying and aggressiveness. These people should always lead a physically active life to allow their pent-up energy full rein.

Mars in Taurus: Physically strong and remarkably enduring. Even if not in a prominent position will add girth and solidity to the subject's frame. Usually attracted to the earth and nature-orientated sports such as rambling, rock climbing or mountaineering, or to sports involving stamina, such as rugby or boxing. Highly sensual, but rigid and stubborn and can be cruel when the energy is used negatively.

Mars in Gemini: Hyperactivity, neuroticism and lack of physical stamina are common with this placement. Intelligent and talkative, however, they crave constant communication – in fact it may be difficult for anybody else to get a word in edgeways. They are attracted to mind games such as chess or bridge, and any occupations involving swift, skilful reactions. They prefer to talk about their physical needs rather than act them out.

Mars in Cancer: Regarded as a difficult position for this fiery planet, the energy being swamped with emotionalism, sensitivity and over-protectiveness. Their nurturing instincts can be too strong at times, but their sexually magnetic natures assure that they will never be short of amorous advances. Water sports, especially swimming or scuba-diving, will attract them.

Mars in Leo: The dare-devil exhibitionists of the zodiac, whose egos inspire them to reach the top in whatever they attempt. They are attracted to anything involving speed and excitement, such as car or speed-boat racing, but in common with their namesake, the lion, they also possess a surprisingly lazy streak and enjoy basking in the sun. As with all the fixed signs, this position of Mars can lead to cruelty, aggression or violence if not channelled properly.

Mars in Virgo: The assertive energy of Mars finds it difficult to prosper in this small-thinking sign – a situation which leads to much carping or criticism, and over concern with health, hygiene or diet on the part of the subject. A good position, however, for the healing profession, both orthodox and alternative. Fast, earthy sports, such as football, tennis, cricket will appeal, but the incentive to exert physical energy is often lacking.

Mars in Virgo: The competitive energy of Mars is somewhat depleted. Preference is shown for mental or creative endeavours, although air sports such as hang-gliding or

ABOVE ALTERNATIVE THERAPIES, SUCH AS MASSAGE, MAY APPEAL TO PEOPLE WITH MARS IN VIRGO.

parachuting will appeal. Usually inoffensive and charming, these people are well-liked, but possess the strange knack of attracting the qualities they dislike most – disharmony and aggression, possibly by their extreme indecisiveness and love of justice.

Mars in Scorpio: Extremely powerful, yet one of the most difficult positions for Mars. The deep intense level of their desires and emotions, renders it difficult for these people to remain composed. Feelings of hate, jealousy, aggression or vindictiveness are therefore easily aroused. These subjects make marvellous, loyal friends, but vengeful enemies. They are highly sexed, determined and excelling in sporting activity.

Mars in Sagittarius: Situated here, the abundant energy of Mars instils its subjects with extreme restlessness. These people will talk with great enthusiasm about anything, impress others with their marvellous physical skills – athletics, archery and horse-riding are amongst their favourites – and keep you laughing with their tremendous sense of humour, but they can be remarkably thick-skinned and insensitive to the feelings of others. Constancy and loyalty are not very high on their list of priorities.

Mars in Capricorn: Mars is exalted in this sign, enabling the energy to be used practically, cautiously and methodically, but the hardness of this configuration renders it difficult for the subject to use sensitivity and balance in his judgement. He can be officious, ambitious, hardworking, calculating, sensual and sly with good business or financial acumen. Slow sports requiring high concentration, such as bowls or snooker, appeal, as do earthy activities such as mountaineering.

Mars in Aquarius: Independent, intelligent, strong-willed and highly individualistic, this position of Mars endows its subjects with an abundance of mental energy with which to pursue a great variety of creative outlets. These subjects are undeniably loyal, friendly and likeable providing they get their own way, but they can be verbally abusive or extremely haughty if thwarted in their aims. Air sports, and games involving speed and skill appeal greatly, and for an air sign they possess surprising physical prowess.

Mars in Pisces: This is a difficult position for Mars, because much of the energy is emotionally diffused. In this sign Mars can become a leech, using martyrdom, guilt and passion as its tools. Direction in life is often difficult thereby resulting in addiction, alcoholism or immoral attitudes. On a more positive level, Mars in Pisces can produce compassion and saintly deeds. Psychic abilities are strong and should be controlled. Water sports and football appeal.

JUPITER

With Jupiter, the largest and most gaseous planet in our solar system, we begin to veer away from the personalization of the first five planets. Jupiter rules our desire to expand, be it mentally or physically, and is usually regarded as a positive influence. It can, however, open up and make worse any difficulties arising in the birth chart and is therefore not always the great benefic it is renowned to be.

Jupiter in Aries: Expands the need for domination, excitement, adventure, conquest and physical needs. Adds extrovertism, brashness, impulsiveness and speed to the character. Self-centred, innovative and basically lucky.

Jupiter in Taurus: Adds solidity, materialism, earthiness, stability, musical ability, and an innate love of the earth. Dependable, financially secure, and sensual, fire-ruled Jupiter is strangely at ease in this heavy earth sign.

Jupiter in Gemini: The expansive qualities of Jupiter are difficult to control in this light air sign. Too much knowledge can be accumulated in a chaotic fashion, causing communication problems. Intelligent, highly verbose and multitalented.

Jupiter in Cancer: Usually kind, sensitive and compassionate, these people possess excellent nurturing instincts and good financial prowess, but can be over-possessive, highly emotional and too concerned with home affairs. Weight may be a problem for these people.

Jupiter in Leo: This configuration usually commands great respect and is considered very fortunate. Loyal, dignified and honest, these people possess a tremendous capacity to give, but sometimes their love of luxury, adornment and riches undermines their innate generosity. They are theatrical, magnetic and physically strong.

ABOVE JUPITER IN CANCER PRODUCES PEOPLE WITH A STRONG CARING INSTINCT.

67

Jupiter in Virgo: Jupiter finds it difficult to blossom within this sign. Expansion is limited, fussy and detailed. Projects are logical and commendable, but rarely able to succeed due to lack of grandeur, and the necessary implementation. Good practical ability, however.

Jupiter in Libra: Finesse, good judgement, charm and success are to be found with this placement. Justice, law and order will attract, as will music, art and drama. Considered a beneficial position for Jupiter, but excessive weight gain and prevarication are two problems which may arise.

Jupiter in Scorpio: Intense and dedicated, passionate and probing, Jupiter here does not like to leave anything untouched once the interest has been aroused. Good financial judgement and keen absorption of knowledge and human nature. Can, however, be over-sexed, possessive and aggressive if the emotions are allowed too much sway.

Jupiter in Sagittarius: In the sign that it rules, Jupiter revels in its freedom and cognition of the world. Optimism, faith, humour, love of variety and learning are all strongly featured within this individual. Sometimes, though, they can go overboard with their enthusiasm to the cost of everything else and lose much of what they value or cherish.

Jupiter in Capricorn: A hard, unpretentious worker, with good sound practical sense. Ambitious and determined, yet able to wait for the right moment to advance, Jupiter positioned here can do much to open up the normally reserved Capricorn character.

Jupiter in Aquarius: A love of freedom combined with great mental ability. These subjects are friendly and outgoing with a projection of warmth normally lacking in the detached Aquarian. Eccentric, individualistic manner, incorporating much talent and ability. Dedication to causes and group activities.

Jupiter in Pisces: The old ruler of Pisces is still very much in tune with this sign and tends to bring out its best qualities – sensitivity, compassion, creativity, imagination, healing ability, saintliness, religious interests, etc., thereby making its subjects more able to cope with the realities of life.

SATURN

Totally opposite in its characteristics to Jupiter, Saturn is supposedly restrictive, fearsome and cold, but it is also life's greatest teacher. We all have to learn, and if we accept the wisdom and discipline of Saturn its energy becomes positive and beneficial, rather than frustrating and depressive.

Saturn in Aries: Not an easy position for Saturn; Aries likes action but Saturn demands caution. The subject desires prominence, freedom and self-assertiveness, often becoming aggressive when seeking his own path, but Saturn here is warning of a need for more patience, and less impulsiveness. All too often these people will act first, then think and regret later. They see themselves as victimized and burdened by responsibilities, and unable to progress in life. When they learn to control their own selfish urges they will automatically become respected.

Saturn in Taurus: Saturn copes well here – both sign and planet are slow in movement and serious in nature. The subject may, however, feel inferior, dull, and lifeless when compared with brighter individuals, and find it difficult to be light-hearted or optimistic, often placing too much value on financial security. Some of these subjects work hard all their lives with seemingly little reward but others become victims of the Taurean laziness and lead very stagnant lives. They need to learn to accept themselves as practical, useful and hardworking members of the community, whereupon their material needs will become less important.

Saturn in Gemini: The restrictions, fears and frustrations experienced by these people are usually all in the mind. They imagine they

LEFT A LOVE OF COMMUNICATION THROUGH WRITING OR TEACHING CAN BE FOUND IN PEOPLE WITH SATURN IN GEMINI.

cannot communicate, or talk as freely as they wish, but in reality they are the opposite, often burdening others with their pessimistic outlook and loquacious tongue. Mental and psychosomatic problems therefore frequently occur. When Saturn in Gemini gains confidence, stops looking on the bleak side and comes to terms with its own unique brand of communication, either by conversing, writing or teaching, the doubts and depression fade into the distance forever.

Saturn in Cancer: This position of Saturn bestows its subjects with excellent nurturing abilities, making them marvellous parents and home-makers. In youth, however, they often deny these needs, appearing to be hard, insensitive and calculating. They may fear the responsibilities of a home and family and seek solace within their own inner world. When they finally accept themselves as normal human beings with strong, sensitive emotions and caring instincts, they become pillars of society. If they marry and endeavour to raise a family before accepting themselves, it can create a very difficult home environment.

Saturn in Leo: The fun loving, flamboyant characteristics of Leo are deeply ingrained within this individual, but rarely able to flow freely. The serious, heavy nature of Saturn overshadows the Leo exhibitionism, especially during youth, causing these people to project themselves quietly when they would prefer to be thrust into the limelight. They often fear ridicule and rejection so much that they will remain in the background until they are totally confident of their reception. When they learn that it is far more rewarding to be spontaneous they quickly become aware of the captivated, adulating audience which awaits them.

Saturn in Virgo: This configuration can work quite well. Both planet and sign love detail and conscientious, practical work. Saturn here is capable of great learning, but the extreme introversion of this combination incites

LEFT PEOPLE WITH SATURN IN VIRGO CAN BE VERY INTROSPECTIVE AND SUFFER FROM ANXIETY.

INTERPRETATION: PLANETS IN SIGNS

intimidation, insecurity and fearfulness. Strong depression and pessimism can also occur, and although over-critical themselves, the slightest amount of criticism from others easily dissuades them from using their tremendous potential. However, when they come to terms with the fact that although they are basically shy, logical and practical, they are in no way inferior to anybody else, and can excel in anything they attempt.

Saturn in Libra: Regarded as one of the better positions for Saturn, being in exaltation (*See* chapter 8), but in reality this is not always the case. The positive qualities of Libra – charm, diplomacy, harmony, justness and finesse – are often hidden when Saturn falls here. The subject fears being too nice, and will purposefully repress his pleasant characteristics, often being rude or dogmatic in the process. When he finally learns that nobody is going to take advantage of him or defile his talents, when he endeavours to be pleasant, affable and charming, he will command respect, being much sought after for his knowledge and advice.

Saturn in Scorpio: The person with Saturn here is terrified of showing his feelings. Emotions are continuously denied, even though his heart craves an outlet. He may also deny his powerful sexuality and feelings of jealousy or resentment, eventually resulting in a torrent of pent-up feelings being expelled in a very aggressive manner. This person is sensitive to everything around him but he may appear cold, ruthless, and utterly heartless until he learns to let go of his emotions in a loving, sensitive manner. If he can do so – which is a tall order, because no other sign finds it quite so difficult to adapt and change as Scorpio – he will be loved and cherished throughout his life.

Saturn in Sagittarius: The Sagittarian urge for freedom and change is hindered with Saturn here. The subject feels unable to allow the adventurous, resourceful side of his nature full rein. He limits his natural optimism and lively temperament and can become melancholic or depressive. He fears showing enthusiasm and will suppress his natural desire to learn and acquire knowledge by demeaning himself. As always, with Saturn, maturity (which can arrive at any age) is the key to the unlocking of the door. When Saturn in Sagittarius decides to open up, speak and say the truth, express his urge to travel and learn, and realize his capabilities, he will go far both mentally and physically.

Saturn in Capricorn: Placed within the sign that it rules Saturn works well, although it does endow its subjects with a serious nature and strong materialistic ideals. These people can also become too enmeshed in the practical side of life, being unable to see the wood for the trees. Single-minded dedication, determination, loyalty and steadiness are all good qualities when used openly without fear, but too often the subject will use these qualities solely for his own use, until such time when they are no longer needed, then discard them from his life quite ruthlessly. The lesson here for these people is to learn to give themselves and their capabilities simply and honestly, without using others or desiring something in return.

Saturn in Aquarius: The old ruler of this sign tends to bring out the more serious contemplative characteristics of the sign, the innate desire for independence and excitement being quelled. The subjects will conform but in a resentful manner, feeling restricted by imagined burdens and responsibilities. Sometimes they project an unfriendly image – they want to be amicable and sociable but find it difficult to be so. Most of the feelings of limitation are on a mental level because although they are extremely intelligent and able to absorb knowledge well, they can be slow in doing so, and imagine themselves lacking in this respect. They need to learn that in order to be readily accepted as responsible citizens, it is not essential to attain knowledge quickly, or to worry about their dispassionate image.

Saturn in Pisces: The emotions do not flow easily with this configuration. Pisces needs to eliminate its worries, fears and negativity through tears and open displays of emotion and affection, but Saturn here blocks this urge, regarding these responses as immature, and demands sensibility. This combination, therefore, can produce a young person with a very old head upon his shoulders, desperately seeking to be recognized as learned and wise, but not being successful in achieving this status because he has not experienced the traumas of life in the manner demanded by the sign of Pisces. To Saturn's credit, however, the common Piscean traits of addiction, disorientation and immorality are far less likely to occur.

URANUS, NEPTUNE AND PLUTO

These three planets take a long-time to transit one sign and are regarded exerting their influence over a generation. In interpreting the birth chart, therefore, their sign position is less significant than their house position. Very briefly, however, they can be interpreted within the signs, as follows:

Uranus in Aries: Galvanizing, exciting, magnetic, highly abrasive, impulsive, and self-centred.

Uranus in Taurus: De-structuralizing, uniquely talented, unusual singing voice, strong tempered.

Uranus in Gemini: Extremely excitable, intelligent, mentally alert, moody, hyperactive.

Uranus in Cancer: Disruptive home and family life, has gifted children, detached emotions, sulky and wilful.

Uranus in Leo: Magnanimous, eccentric, highly effusive, rebellious, remarkable achievements.

Uranus in Virgo: Difficulty in controlling mental and practical outlets. Overloaded mental system. Neurotic.

Uranus in Libra: Unique charm, distant and cold, flair for design and form sudden change of opinion.

Uranus in Scorpio: Dynamic, cruel or vindictive, unusual sexual responses, natural leader, hypnotic physical appeal.

Uranus in Sagittarius: An explorer, highly intelligent bordering upon genius, crazy, insensitive, self-absorbed.

Uranus in Capricorn: Far-seeing, highly ambitious, cold, ruthless, mechanically or practically talented.

Uranus in Aquarius: Inventive, scientific, eccentric, rebellious, non-conformist.

Uranus in Pisces: Highly gifted, powerful imagination, disruptive emotions, moody, unreliable, mentally unstable.

Neptune in Aries: Dominant leadership qualities used in a hypnotic manner. Disorientation whilst travelling. Head illnesses or disorders.

Neptune in Taurus: Artistic, musical, beautiful, living in a fantasy world, a financial disaster.

Neptune in Gemini: Unstable, visionary, head in the clouds, erratic, changeable, gifted.

Neptune in Cancer: Extremely psychic or intuitive water loving. Confused home-life, ultra-sensitive.

Neptune in Leo: Tremendous acting potential, generous, charitable, artistic, magnetic, unstable.

Neptune in Virgo: Becomes confused over small details, untidy, mentally brilliant but chaotic mind, lacks vision.

Neptune in Libra: Love of harmony, beauty and peace. Creative or artistic, extremely indecisive, easily swayed, searching for ideal love.

Neptune in Scorpio: Deep, confused emotions, lack of control, potential for vice or addiction, extremely psychic, imaginative and erotic.

Neptune in Sagittarius: Enthusiasm diffused, a loner or wanderer, unsettled mentally and physically, amorous.

Neptune in Capricorn: Visionary and artistic in a practical manner. Lack of structure in life, highly sensual, disorganized.

Neptune in Aquarius: Vague, dream-like, evasive, devotion to human rights, mentally unstable.

Neptune in Pisces: Great empathy, compassion and sensitivity, a dreamer, saintly, sacrificial, magnetic, not of this world or unable to cope with life's realities.

Pluto in Aries: Volcanic, aggressive, a born leader, heated passion, love of power and control.

Pluto in Taurus: Strong will-power, violent temper, intense love of the land, utterly reliable.

Pluto in Gemini: Powerful manner of speech or communication, volatile, sadistic, highly intelligent.

Pluto in Cancer: Over-protective, possessive and jealous. Deep-rooted emotions. Trauma in early family life.

Pluto in Leo: Obsessive desire to be noticed, magnetic leadership qualities, strong-willed, controlling.

Pluto in Virgo: Obsessive about hygiene. Powerful sex-drive, capable of great detail, worries about minor details of life.

Pluto in Libra: Charming in a powerful, hypnotic manner, thrives on admiration, aggressive in pursuit of justice.

Pluto in Scorpio: Intense feelings of every kind, violent temper, uneasy childhood, destructive, wilful, psychic, marvellous memory.

Pluto in Sagittarius: Tremendous urge to travel, intense about learning, prophetic, powerful leader, quick tempered.

Pluto in Capricorn: Strong sense of duty and responsibility, feelings of being overburdened. Sensual and manipulating.

Pluto in Aquarius: Highly individualistic, intense about scientific, computerized age, unfeeling, dominant.

Pluto in Pisces: Emotions experienced with deep intensity, prone to the very worst in addiction, self-destructive, powerful healer, extremist.

75

RIGHT PLUTO IN SAGITTARIUS CAN PRODUCE

PEOPLE WHO ARE INTENSE ABOUT LEARNING.

INTERPRETATION: PLANETS IN HOUSES

I t is now time to move on to the most fascinating, yet often the most neglected part of astrological interpretation – the houses. There are many different methods of house division but the system used within this book – the Equal House system, which contains 12 equally proportioned houses of 30 degrees, as represented in our diagrams in chapter 5 – is the most ancient, simple and balanced method of all.

THE HOUSES

The houses can be divided into three groups as follows:
- Angular – 1st, 4th, 7th and 10th.
- Succedent – 2nd, 5th, 8th and 11th.
- Cadent – 3rd, 6th, 9th and 12th.

Planets situated in the angular houses appear to have more impact upon the birth chart and are therefore regarded as being very important, especially when placed within an 8 degree orb of the relevant house cusp. Generally speaking planets in angular houses initiate situations that are then implemented by the planets in succedent houses, to be finally improved or modified by the planets in cadent houses.

Each house is representative of a certain area of life, and a planet situated within a house will give this 'area' importance.

Ascendant/First house: The sign on the cusp (beginning) of the first house is always the Ascendant (Rising Sign), and as such is the main indicator of the outer personality, the appearance and the immediate impact projection of the subject upon others.

Second house: Financial and monetary concerns, earning potential, possessions, values, lower senses, appetite.

Third house: Daily mundane activity, childhood education, short-distance travel, all relatives other than parents, writing, teaching, general communication.

Fourth house: One of the parents, usually the father. Home and private life, hereditary factors, inner emotions.

Fifth house: Creativity, children, sports, hobbies, romantic attachments, gambling, social instinct.

Sixth house: Work environment, service given and received, health interests, small animals or pets.

Seventh house: Marital or business relationships, childhood friendships, open enemies or conflict.

Eighth home: Birth, death, inheritance, partner's monetary concerns, sexuality, psychic and spiritual interests.

Ninth house: Long-distance travel, higher learning, religion, philosophy, teaching.

Tenth house: Aims, ambitions and fulfilment. One of the parents, usually the mother.

Eleventh house: Friends, groups and societies, social activity.

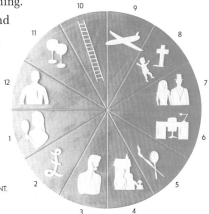

RIGHT EACH OF THE 12 HOUSES REPESENTS A SPECIFIC AREA OF OUR LIFE AND A PLANET SITUATED WITHIN A PARTICULAR HOUSE WILL MAKE THIS AREA IMPORTANT.

Twelfth house: Hospitals, prisons, charities, large institutions, guilts, secrets, sorrows, self-destruction, religious and spiritual concerns.

When analysing the planets in the houses we are interpreting the area of life in which the planet requires expression. The following gives a brief example of how the ten planets might be expressed in each house.

SUN

First: The ego and individuality are directed towards the self, giving a strong personality with much egotism, self-centredness and pride.

Second: The ego and individuality are directed towards finances, possessions and values. Good earning potential and business ability.

Third: The ego and individuality are directed towards communication of all kinds. A restless nature with a need for learning, commitment to relatives and daily activity.

Fourth: The ego and individuality are directed towards the home. Father will figure strongly in the life. A need for privacy and domestic attachments.

Fifth: The ego and individuality are directed towards creative expression. Children and romantic attachments provide much gratification.

Sixth: The ego and individuality are directed towards work. Beneficial or detrimental to health depending upon aspects. Good rapport with animals.

Seventh: The ego and individuality are directed towards partnerships of all kinds, and can only be expressed clearly when the subject is involved with another person.

ABOVE A PERSON WITH THE SUN IN HIS OR HER FIRST HOUSE WILL HAVE A STRONG PERSONALITY AND TAKE GREAT PRIDE IN THEMSELVES.

Eighth: The ego and individuality are directed towards anything related to or given by other people. Absorbs and holds in emotions for the purpose of ego gratification. Strong passions.

Ninth: The ego and individuality are directed towards higher learning and study and a need for reaching out towards others. Travelling satisfies these urges, as does religious study.

Tenth: The ego and individuality are directed towards ambitions and fulfilment. Needs to be successful in endeavours or prominent within chosen career.

Eleventh: The ego and individuality are directed towards maintaining support from friendships and group activities.

Twelfth: The ego and individuality are directed towards secretiveness, hospitals and institutions. Self-denial, frustrated self-expression or destructive tendencies may be present.

ABOVE A LOVE OF TRAVEL IS COMMON IN PEOPLE WITH THE SUN IN THEIR NINTH HOUSE.

Moon

First: The emotions, habits and responses are expressed openly, via the personality. Physically, the features will either be plump, pale, weak and rounded, or thin, dark, sallow and sharp.

Second: The emotions, habits and responses are readily expressed by a need to nurture financial and material accumulations, and a desire to cling to the past. Earning capacity good, but changeable.

Third: The emotions, habits and responses are expressed during communication. Impressionable, and receptive to learning, with need for security through relatives.

Fourth: The emotions, habits and responses are expressed very privately. Home is extremely important. One parent, usually the mother, is very protective and prominent in the life. Vulnerable, sensitive and intuitive.

Fifth: The emotions, habits and responses are expressed creatively. Strong nurturing instincts towards children, hobbies and creative endeavours. Many romantic attachments.

Sixth: The emotions, habits and responses are expressed through the work environment and an interest in health, hygiene and service. Good attunement with animals.

ABOVE PEOPLE WITH THE MOON IN THEIR FIFTH HOUSE OFTEN POSSESS A STRONG NURTURING INSTINCT.

Seventh: The emotions, habits and responses are expressed powerfully within a meaningful relationship. May desire to be protected and nurtured by a partner or to behave thus towards a partner themselves.

Eighth: The emotions, habits and responses are expressed mainly through sexual or spiritual outlets. Good at handling other people's finances or possessions. Psychic ability.

Ninth: The emotions, habits and responses are expressed intelligently within higher learning, and foreign affairs. Residence abroad is readily accepted and enjoyed. Great interest in philosophies and religions.

Tenth: The emotions, habits and responses are expressed openly with regard to aims and ambitions, often leading to successful public life. Will have a dominant, protective mother.

Eleventh: The emotions, habits and responses are expressed within friendships and group activities. Female friends will predominate. Protective towards friends.

Twelfth: The emotions, habits and responses are expressed with great difficulty, and usually in private. Intuitive, imaginative, lonely, misunderstood and highly secretive these subjects travel life's highway on their own.

MERCURY

First: The urge to communicate is strong and usually centred around the self. Adds liveliness and sparkle to the personality and often a lithesome figure too.

Second: The urge to communicate is centred around materialistic requirements. Good ideas on how to earn money, but no practical implementation.

Third: The urge to communicate is vital in this house. Restless in daily activity with learning capacity. Extremely chatty and knowledgeable if well aspected.

Fourth: The urge to communicate operates mainly within the home environment, with good ideas on home improvement. Will have a communicative, intelligent father.

Fifth: The urge to communicate is represented by creative endeavours and mental activity. Intelligent, lively children. Flirtatious, restless outlook.

Sixth: The urge to communicate is strongly expressed within the working environment, and a knowledge of health interests. Understands animals.

RIGHT THE ABILITY TO COMMUNICATE WITH AND UNDERSTAND ANIMALS IS A QUALITY ASSOCIATED WITH PEOPLE WITH MERCURY IN THEIR SIXTH HOUSE.

Seventh: The urge to communicate is propelled into relationships. Either the subject or partner will be excessively talkative with self-centred tendencies.

Eighth: The urge to communicate is kept under control, except when concerned with the finances of others, or spiritual matters. Enjoys talking about physical needs.

Ninth: The urge to communicate is channelled into higher learning, religion, philosophies, languages and foreign concerns. Highly intelligent, much-travelled person.

Tenth: The urge to communicate is centred around the ambitions. Successful careers involving communication are common. Influenced greatly by lively mother.

Eleventh: The urge to communicate is focused upon friends and group activities. Lively, versatile and chatty with friends. Enjoys group discussion.

Twelfth: The urge to communicate is repressed and submerged into the imagination, which can then become over active. Mental illness occurs if not used positively. Secretive, delving mind with many unused talents.

LEFT MERCURY IN THE NINTH HOUSE CREATES INTEREST IN FOREIGN CONCERNS.

82

VENUS

First: The desire for love, peace and harmony is conveyed by a charming, pleasant personality. Attractive appearance, but the subject often values himself too highly.

Second: The desire for love, peace and harmony is channelled through materialistic and sensual needs, or through a great love of nature.

Third: The desire for love, peace and harmony is expressed through conversation, writing or artistic endeavours. Good rapport with relatives, siblings and teachers.

Fourth: The desire for love, peace and harmony is exhibited within the home environment. The home and possessions are valued highly. Will have a loving father.

Fifth: The desire for love, peace and harmony is asserted spontaneously through creative endeavours and through a love of children. There a need for romantic liaisons and much social activity.

Sixth: The desire for love, peace and harmony is channelled into maintaining a pleasant working environment and an appreciation of health interests. Love of animals.

Seventh: The desire for love, peace and harmony is extremely strong within relationships. Enjoys giving or receiving love. Attracts good influences from others.

Eighth: The desire for love, peace and harmony is expressed mainly through the physical needs of a relationship. Inheritance, and acquisition of possessions are indicated. Loves deeply.

Ninth: The desire for love, peace and harmony is projected outwardly into study, religion, philosophy, etc. Love of travelling and foreign subjects.

ABOVE GIVING AND RECEIVING LOVE IS IMPORTANT TO PEOPLE WITH VENUS IN THEIR SEVENTH HOUSE.

Tenth: The desire for love, peace and harmony is expressed through the career. Drawn to artistic, feminine careers such as fashion, hairdressing or beauty consultancy. Attractive, charming mother.

Eleventh: The desire for love, peace and harmony is channelled into friendships and beneficial group activities. Charming, artistic friends, with strong materialistic instincts.

Twelfth: The desire for love, peace and harmony is depicted by a need for solitude and meditation. Appreciates hospitals and institutions. May even be happy living a restricted, secluded life.

MARS

First: Energy, drive and enthusiasm radiate from the personality. Aggressiveness may also be apparent. The features will be strong, signifying power and authority.

Second: Energy, drive and enthusiasm are directed into material issues. Excellent earning potential and accumulation of possessions. Overbearing attitudes.

Third: Energy, drive and enthusiasm are channelled into communication. Powerful speaker or writer. Dominance meted out or received from relatives.

Fourth: Energy, drive and enthusiasm are focused upon home affairs. Assertive and dominant in private matters. Powerful, aggressive father and/or difficult upbringing.

Fifth: Energy, drive and enthusiasm are ignited by romantic attachments, children and creative pursuits. Dominant towards children. Sportingly active.

Sixth: Energy, drive and enthusiasm are channelled into work. Interestingly workaholics often possess this position of Mars, with resulting health problems. Dominant or aggressive with animals.

Seventh: Energy, drive and enthusiasm are directed into relationships. Will dominate or be dominated by partner. Arguments occur frequently.

Eighth: Energy, drive and enthusiasm are greatly controlled, but tremendously powerful. Strong sexual urges and an innate ability to accumulate anything from others.

Ninth: Energy, drive and enthusiasm are expelled through learning and travelling. Assertiveness and influential ability is strong. Could be a religious leader.

Tenth: Energy, drive and enthusiasm are directed into ambition and career. The Army, Police Force or any highly physical, male-dominated occupation would appeal. Powerful mother.

Eleventh: Energy, drive and enthusiasm are sustained by powerful friendships. Attracts, or strongly reacts to, assertive, aggressive people or group situations.

Twelfth: Energy, drive and enthusiasm are hidden and difficult to release. Secret physical or sexual prowess. Self-destructive tendencies and great interest in hospital or institutional activities.

JUPITER

First: Expansiveness and optimism are expressed openly in the personality. Height or girth is added to the frame, especially in later years. Likeable person.

Second: Expansiveness and optimism are used in material concerns. Good fortune and earning potential. Tendency to overeat and revel in the luxuries of life.

Third: Expansiveness and optimism are directed towards others. Much beneficial short-distance travel and encouragement from relatives. Thinks and acts big.

ABOVE A LOVE OF LIFE, AND OFTEN FOOD, IS FOUND IN PEOPLE WITH JUPITER IN THEIR SECOND HOUSE.

Fourth: Expansiveness and optimism are discharged within the home. Appreciative of spacious, rambling premises. Beneficial father or genial upbringing.

Fifth: Expansiveness and optimism are shown towards children and romantic attachments, which may be many in number. Lucky gambling instincts. Enjoys social activities.

Sixth: Expansiveness and optimism manifest within working conditions. Likeable working companions. Good health and recuperative powers. Love of large animals.

Seventh: Expansiveness and optimism are projected into partnerships. Elevated or influential partner. General benefits through business or marital relationships.

Eighth: Expansiveness and optimism are directed towards other people's resources. Inheritance and accumulation of possessions likely. Good investigatory powers.

Ninth: Expansiveness and optimism are generated by travel and learning. Religion and philosophy are widely studied. Adds wisdom and positivity to the chart.

Tenth: Expansiveness and optimism are generated through the career. A position of authority, power and respect is desired. Politics, the stock market, acting or teaching should appeal.

Eleventh: Expansiveness and optimism are bestowed upon and received from, friends. Positions of authority within group situations are accorded. Luck through influential friends.

Twelfth: Expansiveness and optimism are witheld from daily activities. Tremendous imagination and capacity for secrets. Hospital, charitable and religious work beneficial.

SATURN

First: Limitation seriousness, fears and lack of confidence are projected into the personality. There is often restriction on weight or growth and/or sallow features.

Second: Limitation, seriousness, fears and lack of confidence are experienced with material concerns, which often leads to parsimony. Restrictions on possessions and appetite. Rigid values.

Third: Limitation, seriousness, fears and lack of confidence are projected through communication, relatives and daily activity. Learning problems and fears regarding transport. Often 'only' or 'lonely' children.

LEFT SATURN IN THE SECOND HOUSE CAN LEAD TO RESTRICTIONS IN A PERSON'S EATING HABITS.

Fourth: Limitation, seriousness, fears and lack of confidence are expressed in the home. Extreme difficulty in showing feelings. Severe, disciplinary or unloving father or lonely upbringing. Good, responsible home-maker.

Fifth: Limitation, seriousness, fears and lack of confidence are revealed in creative endeavours and sporting activities. Harsh with children. Slow to form romantic attachments.

Sixth: Limitation, seriousness, fears and lack of confidence are experienced in work situations. Weak constitution. Either workaholic or afraid of work. May be frightened of animals.

ABOVE A WORKAHOLIC OR WORK-SHY PERSON MAY HAVE SATURN POSITIONED IN THEIR SIXTH HOUSE.

Seventh: Limitation, seriousness, fears and lack of confidence are encountered in relationships. Attraction to older partners – possibly seeking parental substitute. Delays and frustrations within marriage.

87

Eighth: Limitation, seriousness, fears and lack of confidence are suffered within physical relationships. Partners' resources minimal or inadequate. Delays in inheritance. Birth problems in females.

Ninth: Limitation, seriousness, fears and lack of confidence are keenly felt when studying or learning. Travel arrangements thwarted or delayed. Serious and dedicated about religion and principles.

Tenth: Limitation, seriousness, fears and lack of confidence are sustained through the career. Although there is strong ambition, there may be delays in achieving success and fulfilment. Desirous of positions of authority.

Eleventh: Limitation, seriousness, fears and lack of confidence are experienced in group situations. Finds it difficult to relate closely to friends, but loyal and responsible towards them.

Twelfth: Limitation, seriousness, fears and lack of confidence are deeply ingrained but rarely expressed openly. Often feels obligated or responsible for the actions of others. Depression is common.

URANUS

First: Disruption, changeability and eccentricity combine to render an unusual, intelligent and diverse personality, usually with something very striking about the features.

Second: Disruption, changeability and eccentricity are amongst the attitudes projected towards financial status, earning power and values. Brilliant or unusual ideas on how to earn money. Inconsistent values.

Third: Disruption, changeability and eccentricity occur within day-to-day activities. Detached, self-centred relatives. Difficult to educate as a child but extremely bright. Accident-prone when travelling.

Fourth: Disruption, changeability and eccentricity are directed towards the home environment. Many changes of residence. Detached emotions. Uncaring or absent father. Attracted to large, modern decor.

Fifth: Disruption, changeability and eccentricity are channelled into creative outlets, sometimes of a bizarre nature. Unusually gifted but rebellious offspring. Mentally astute with powerful, but erratic physical stamina.

Sixth: Disruption, changeability and eccentricity within the working environment. Difficult co-workers. Losses and change of job. Sudden health problems. Love of unusual or large animals.

Seventh: Disruption, changeability and eccentricity develop during permanent relationships, often causing divorce or

LEFT SOMEONE WHO KEEPS MOVING HOUSE MAY HAVE URANUS IN THEIR FOURTH HOUSE.

separation. Many partners. Either subject or partner will be extremely self-absorbed and independent.

Eighth: Disruption, changeability and eccentricity arise with physical involvement. Unusual sexual desires. Unexpected monetary gains and losses. Detached, unstable emotions. Clever or cunning mind. Occult interests.

Ninth: Disruption, changeability and eccentricity occur when travelling or learning. Changes of religious faith. Brilliant mind. Freedom-seeking. Love of travelling to or learning about exotic, far-away places.

Tenth: Disruption, changeability and eccentricity are channelled into the career, of which there may be more than one, and an independent, mind-absorbing career is desired. Unfortunate, rebellious or unusual mother.

Eleventh: Disruption, changeability and eccentricity are qualities which friends of this subject possess in abundance. Exciting, unusual group situations attract. Many changes or sudden disappearances of friends.

Twelfth: Disruption, changeability and eccentricity become deeply ingrained within the mind of this individual, sometimes leading to mental and emotional problems. Unexpected associations with hospitals or institutions.

NEPTUNE

First: Softness, sensitivity, confusion, and escapism combine to render this person magnetic, ethereal and extremely difficult to understand. Adds a dreamy, far-away look to the features and a round, plump body.

Second: Softness, sensitivity, confusion and escapism are not qualities which auger well for financial success. Losses of money and possessions, or being over-generous or careless with money. Clouded values. Poor appetite.

Third: Softness, sensitivity, confusion and escapism bring about strange events during daily activity. No sense of direction. Mentally confused, disorientated or unhelpful relatives. Lack of concentration in education. Artistic or musical talent.

Fourth: Softness, sensitivity, confusion and escapism create an uneasy homelife with an inability to settle or take root. May have a strange, absent, negligent or idealized father. Unsure of roots. Chaotic and untidy.

Fifth: Softness, sensitivity, confusion and escapism are all projected into creativity endowing the subject with artistic, musical or theatrical talent. May have sensitive or unsettled children. Love of water and liquids, including alcoholic beverages.

Sixth: Softness, sensitivity, confusion and escapism do not make it easy for this person to be confident within a working environment. Strange, undiagnosable health problems. Diabetes or fluid retention a problem. Gentle with animals.

Seventh: Softness, sensitivity, confusion and escapism render it difficult for this subject to find fulfilment within a relationship. Idealization of partner can occur with eventual disappointment. Unreliable for business partnerships and an attraction to weak or deceitful partners.

Eighth: Softness, sensitivity, confusion and escapism are readily contained and controlled with this placement. Highly emotional and passionate with powerful intuitive faculties. Disappointment through the financial affairs of others, and losses of inheritance or possessions.

Ninth: Softness, sensitivity, confusion and escapism do not blend well into this area. Devoted to religious causes, but can easily be used by stronger people. Travel by sea and studies of a spiritual nature should appeal.

Tenth: Softness, sensitivity, confusion and escapism cause problems of indecision, lack of attainment and self-assertion in this area. Suited to careers of an artistic, musical or theatrical nature. Although there is a yearning for recognition, escapist tendencies shun the limelight.

Eleventh: Softness, sensitivity, confusion and escapism render this person kind, sympathetic and helpful towards friends, and prone to attracting lame dogs or weak people. Occult, spiritual or religious groups should appeal. Unable to handle responsibility within groups.

Twelfth: Softness, sensitivity, confusion and escapism are hidden qualities of this subject. Neptune copes well in its natural house. Attracted to hospitals and institutions or anything spiritual. Powerful imagination. Regarded as an 'old soul'.

PLUTO

First: Power, authority and magnetism ooze from this subject's personality, sometimes rendering them overbearing and debilitating to others. Tenacity, determination and intensity of features, especially the eyes, will set them apart from the crowd.

Second: Power, authority and magnetism are channelled into earning capacity and financial success. Dedicated to values and prone to obsessive needs, they do not let go of anything with ease.

Third: Power, authority and magnetism are directed towards or received from relatives. Daily activity undertaken with serious, intense concentration. Absorbs information slowly but deeply. Possible traumatic loss of siblings.

Fourth: Power, authority and magnetism are used within the home. Likes to rule the roost. Possible early loss of father. Obsessive about home and emotions. Does not take readily to changes of abode.

Fifth: Power, authority and magnetism are exerted over children and loved ones. Strong sexual appeal. Although thorough and intense over creative pursuits, the subject is not very adventurous or adaptable. Possible loss of children.

Sixth: Power, authority and magnetism are projected into work situations. Likes to hold positions of respect and command. Extremely capable with animals. Traumatic losses of job. Intense about health, but likely to suffer from growths, or sexual diseases.

BELOW SUBJECTS WITH PLUTO IN THEIR SIXTH HOUSE ARE PRONE TO BEING VERY HEALTH CONSCIOUS.

Seventh: Power, authority and magnetism are used by one of the partners within a relationship. Traumatic divorce, loss or separation often occurs. Intrinsically loyal and in much need of a firm, steady relationship. Good for business partnerships.

Eighth: Power, authority and magnetism are well controlled in this house. Strong sexual urges, and an innate fascination for the life/birth/death process, and anything to do with the underworld. Immense gains or losses through inheritance.

Ninth: Power, authority and magnetism are concentrated into higher learning, religion and travel. Capable of tremendous dedication. Potential for

LEFT RELIGION MATTERS TO PEOPLE WITH PLUTO IN THE NINTH HOUSE.

religious leader. May end life in a foreign country or become intense about foreign concerns.

Tenth: Power, authority and magnetism are used within the career. Strongly ambitious with a need for control over others. Good business sense. Careers involving stamina and dedication are suitable. Powerful, dominant mother.

Eleventh: Power, authority and magnetism are projected onto friends and group situations. Desires commanding position within group. Loyal and dependable, yet difficult to approach. Loss of friends.

Twelfth: Power, authority and magnetism are qualities that this subject will only project in his imagination. Intuitive and deep, with a need for some kind of association with hospitals, institutions or prisons, this person is inwardly a loner.

INTERPRETATION: OTHER CONFIGURATIONS

The signs, houses and aspects are the most influential factors of chart interpretation, but there are many other significant components that can be applied. In this chapter we are going to become acquainted with the most important of these factors.

CHART SHAPING

This system of dividing the chart wheel into various distinct types of shapings was originally devised by Marc Edmund Jones and explained in his book *The Guide to Horoscope Interpretation*, which was first published in 1941. Since then it has become an integral part of most astrologers' preliminary interpretation. Below are descriptions of the original seven shapings.

BUNDLE

A very intense shaping with all planets being contained within 120 degrees, and four or five houses. It gives tenacity, determination and single-minded attitudes to the areas and signs that it occupies. It is more insular and concerned with personal affairs when in the lower half of the chart and more concerned with public affairs when placed in the upper portion of the chart.

LEFT A BUNDLE CONFIGURATION GIVES THE SUBJECT DETERMINATION AND SINGLEMINDEDNESS IN THE AREAS THAT THE PLANETS OCCUPY.

BOWL

Again a somewhat restricted shaping, all the planets being confined within 180 degrees (one half of the chart). When placed within the lower section of the chart (houses 1–6), the subject is more likely to be introverted, lacking in confidence and concerned with private affairs, but when placed in the upper half of the chart (houses 7–12), the subject is usually extroverted and confident in public, but finds it difficult to relate on a personal level. If all the planets are placed on the ascending half of the chart (houses 10–3) the subject is self-contained and independent, with leadership qualities, but when placed in the opposite half (houses 4–9), the subject is more dependent and often forced to follow the dictates of others.

ABOVE IN HOUSES 7-12, THE BOWL CONFIGURATION CAN INDCATE EXTROVERTISM AND CONFIDENCE IN PUBLIC MATTERS.

BUCKET

Very similar to the Bowl, except that one planet (or occasionally, a conjunction of planets) is situated in the opposite sphere of the chart, allowing a route into the 'other side of the world'. For example, the

introvert with nine of his planets in the lower half of the chart, but with Mars in the tenth, is able to emerge from his shell in the sphere of life relating to career and ambition. Conversely, the subject with nine planets in the top half of the chart and one in the fourth, is allowed an access into the personal area of home. The singleton planet is always an extremely important focal point in a person's life.

ABOVE THE SINGLE PLANET IN THE BUCKET CONFIGURATION ALLOWS A PERSON ACCESS TO 'THE OTHER SIDE' OF HIS CHARACTER.

LOCOMOTIVE

All the planets are situated within 240 degrees (the space of two trines) with the remaining 120 degrees empty. As its name implies, the subject with this shaping has a self-driving personality. The planet leading (pulling) the group in a clockwise direction is said to be the most significant and indicative of the manner in which the subject instigates action, but the planet at the opposite end which appears to be at the rear of the train can often be just as important, especially if it is stronger than the leading planet.

ABOVE A LOCOMOTIVE PERSON IS USUALLY DRIVEN IN THE AREA OF THEIR LIFE REPRESENTED BY THE PLANET LEADING THE GROUP (TRAVELLING IN A CLOCKWISE DIRECTION).

SEESAW

A shaping which has become uncommon over the last few decades, mainly due to the outer planets aligning themselves close together and rendering it much more difficult for this shape to form.

As the name suggests, the planets are divided into two relatively even groups, one in each half of the chart, usually creating several opposition aspects. This shaping causes a permanent striving for balance, which is rarely achieved because, like the motion of the seesaw, the subject veers from one extreme to the other. For example, an extrovert with a need of public recognition (five or six planets in the ninth and tenth) can swiftly change into an introvert with a desperate need for privacy and the mundane achievements of life (opposing planets in the third and fourth).

ABOVE A PERSON WITH TWO EVEN GROUPS OF PLANETS ON OPPOSITE SIDES OF THEIR CHART MAY FIND THEMSELVES VEERING FROM ONE EXTREME TO ANOTHER.

SPLASH

In contrast to the first five shapings, the Splash shaping reveals planets (usually singletons, but conjunctions are also allowable) dotted all over the chart, leaving very few empty houses. The subject with this shaping tends to scatter his or her interests, being very talented and capable, but also finding it difficult to concentrate. This is similar in effect to the sign of Gemini and the mutable influence). However, because most of the signs, houses, elements, etc., are occupied there is usually much balance, knowledge and understanding of life.

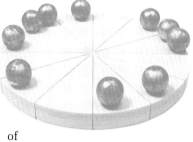

ABOVE A SPLASH SHAPE CAN LEAD TO A PERSON SCATTERING THEIR INTERESTS, ALTHOUGH A BALANCE IS USUALLY ACHIEVED AS MOST HOUSES ARE OCCUPIED A PLANET.

SPLAY

Often difficult to differentiate from the Splash, which is similar in appearance. The Splay forms an irregular, uneven type of shaping which tends to occupy a fair amount of the chart. The subject with this shaping finds it difficult or impossible to conform, is independent, unusual and often wilful (the effect can be likened to the planet Uranus or the sign Aquarius).

MC (MIDHEAVEN), IC (IMMUM COELI) AND DESCENDANT

These three points plus the Ascendant, which are calculated according to the time of birth and the position of the Ascendant, form an imaginary cross within the circle of the natal birth chart. The Midheaven (MC) is by far the most important and is regarded as the highest point (a pinnacle of great achievement or satisfaction) within the birth chart. When using the House system explained within this book, the Midheaven can fall anywhere between the 8th and 11th houses, but more commonly it falls within the 9th or 10th houses.

The Immum Coeli (IC) is the point which falls in exact opposition to the Midheaven and is therefore regarded as the lowest, innermost part of the chart. It can fall anywhere between the second and fifth houses, but more commonly in the third or fourth. The Descendant is always the (beginning) of the seventh house, and therefore falls at the point exactly opposite the Ascendant (cusp of the first house). Whereas the Ascendant relates entirely to the self, the Descendant depicts how the subject relates to others in close relationships.

RULING PLANET

The planet which rules the sign on the Ascendant is termed as the ruling planet of the chart and is therefore extremely important. A subject may often present a physical appearance more typical of the sign in which the ruler of the chart is placed than the Ascendant itself. For example, with Gemini on the Ascendant and the ruler Mercury placed in Cancer, the appearance may take on many overtones of a Cancerian. If the ruling planet is in conjunction with another planet, that planet too may affect the appearance. The personality can also be greatly affected by the position of the ruler, and the aspects it makes. If placed in an angular house it may dominate the whole chart. A person with a very extroverted sign such as Leo rising will be more subdued within their personality if the Sun (ruler) falls in a passive sign, whereas a passive, introverted sign rising with the ruler placed in an active sign will generally produce a more confident, outgoing personality. The area of life in which the ruler of the chart falls is highly important and will always be prominent or esteemed.

ANGULAR PLANETS

Any planet falling within an 8 degree orb on either side of an angular house, can be termed 'angular'. This includes planets which are situated at the end of the 3rd, 6th, 9th and 12th houses. For example, a planet situated at 3 degrees of Aquarius in the 3rd house, with the cusp of the 4th at 10 degrees of Aquarius, will still be angular.

Angular planets should be studied carefully, especially when they make many aspects, as they can dominate a chart. They are often indicative of the whole life-style of the subject. For example, Mars angular produces physically active people such as athletes, whereas Neptune angular produces musicians, actors, escapists, addicts, etc.

STELLIUMS

A group of three or more planets positioned within one sign or one house is called a 'stellium'. Such a high concentration of planets in one area always indicates tremendous strength, and can therefore govern the chart. The strength may not necessarily be used positively, especially if there are many difficult aspects involved, and the excess of activity within a confined area can often prove to be very difficult to handle.

PLANETS IN EXALTATION, DETRIMENT AND FALL

The original seven planets are traditionally considered to be exalted (well-placed) when posited in certain signs, as follows:

☉ is exalted in	♈
☽ is exalted in	♉
☿ is exalted in	♍
♀ is exalted in	♓
♂ is exalted in	♑
♃ is exalted in	♋
♄ is exalted in	♎

When these same planets are placed in the signs opposite those above they are considered to be in their 'fall' (weakly placed). For example, the Sun is in its fall in Libra.

A planet is described as being in detriment when placed in the sign opposite to that which it rules. For example, Venus rules both Taurus and Libra and is therefore in detriment (badly placed) when in the signs of Scorpio and Aries. A planet in its own sign, however, is considered to be strong.

RETROGRADE PLANETS

When retrograde, planets appear to be moving backwards when seen from an earth perspective and this apparent motion backwards is obviously at the root of the belief that retrograde planets are less effective within a birth chart than those which are moving direct. (Note: The Sun and Moon never turn retrograde.) This assumption seems to possess little credibility, especially with the outer planets which, because they move so slowly, are often retrograde for great periods. It has been noted, however, that when Mercury turns retrograde delays, frustrations and confusion over all Mercurial concerns seem to occur. Post is delayed, transport is inefficient, and daily communication may be beset with problems. People with Mercury retrograde in their birth chart frequently possess some kind of communication problem. Venus retrograde often finds it difficult to love, and Mars retrogade may have problems in expelling energy. It is therefore well worth noting when these three personal planets are retrograde within a birth chart.

MAJOR PLANETARY CONFIGURATIONS

These consist of various groupings of several major aspects as follows:

THE 'T' SQUARE ○─○

This involves a combination of two squares and an opposition, the two planets involved in the opposition both being square to the third planet, which forms the 'T'. It is a very common configuration, renowned for its difficulty and lack of ease in operating. The subjects are often very

ABOVE PEOPLE WITH A 'T' SQUARE GROUP MAY BE TENSE IN THE AREAS OCCUPIED IN THE PLANETS.

tense and lacking in fulfilment within the areas occupied by the planets. Much hard work and understanding is required in order to render the configuration harmonious and productive in its energy. Three or more planets can be involved, but if more than three, there must be at least one close conjunction of two or more of the planets.

THE GRAND TRINE △

A combination of three trines involving three or more planets (more than three planets must also involve a conjunction of at least two planets), usually within the same element, form this major figure. Regarded as being highly beneficial and easy to operate, it also appears to add charm, lightness and talent to the birth chart. As with all trines,

♃ 19°

♆ 18°

☿ 12°

ABOVE THE GRAND TRINE IS CONSIDERED AS A BENEFICIAL CONFIGURATION WHICH ADDS CHARM AND EVEN TALENT TO A BIRTH CHART.

however, there is a tendency for inertia or acceptance, thereby nullifying the tremendous advantages of the configuration.

THE GRAND CROSS +

Far less common than the 'T' Square and Grand Trine, this powerful configuration involves at least four planets combined in four squares and two oppositions and forming an imaginary cross shape upon the chart. With six difficult aspects involved, it is inevitably an extremely problematical configuration to conquer and use wisely. It often brings tremendous conflicts and difficulties into the lives of its owners, becoming even more potent when angular or placed in the angular

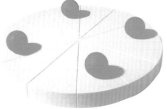

LEFT WITH AT LEAST SIX ASPECTS INVOLVED, THE GRAND CROSS OFTEN BRINGS CONFLICTS AND DIFFICULTIES INTO THE LIVES OF ITS SUBJECTS.

houses. The subjects tend to make the same mistakes over and over again. They easily become obsessed, aggressive and rebellious, or depressed, escapist and self-abasing, according to the planets and signs involved. However, once the awesome power of this configuration is harnessed, controlled and chanelled in the right direction, there is very little that the subject cannot achieve.

THE YOD ▷

Also known as the Finger of God, this is the least common of the four major configurations. It involves two quincunxes and a sextile, the two planets creating the sextile both making a quincunx to the third planet, and thereby forming a pointed finger shape. The planet involved in the two quincunxes is considered to be the focal point of release for the other two planets, its skill and talents being better utilized with the aid of the remaining two planets. Occasionally one or more extra planets are involved in this configuration, but as both the quincunx and sextile use smaller orbs than the aspects involved in the other configurations, it is quite a rare phenomenon. The Yod does seem to indicate a 'special' gift or talent which should be used by the individual, but in common with the quincunx aspect the talent may not be apparent, or utilized until much adjustment has been made and time elapsed. The configuration usually occurs in the chart of highly developed, or spiritual individuals.

103

RIGHT AN UNCOMMON CONFIGURATION,
THE YOD BESTOWS BOTH ADVERSITY AND
CREATIVITY UPON PEOPLE, OFTEN LEADING
TO A DEEP SPIRITUALITY IN LATE LIFE.

PREDICTIVE ASTROLOGY

Moving on from the analysis of a birth chart, the next step is to learn about the predictive element of astrology (the effect of the continuous movement of the planets upon our lives). There are many alternative methods of prognosis, but this chapter will deal purely with the two traditionally esteemed methods – Progressions and Transits, for which you will require a copy of an ephemeris which runs up to the year 2000.

PROGRESSIONS

A relatively simple, precise method of prediction in which the personal planets of the Sun, Moon, Mercury, Venus and Mars play the vital role. These planets are progressed within the ephemeris 'a day for each year' in the following manner.

Turn to the relevant date of birth in the ephemeris. Then count down each day until you arrive at the day which corresponds to the actual age, moving onto the following month or page, if necessary. For example, for 16 years of age count on 16 days, for 50 years of age count on 50 days. The planet's positions on this new date are the progressed positions for the birthday of the year in question, but they require minor adjustments before being used for predictive purposes.

To demonstrate we shall use our second example, who was born at 9.40pm Greenwich Mean Time on 6 July 1941. To find out the progressed planet's positions for this subject upon attaining the age of 21, count down 21 days from 6 July to arrive at the date of 27 July, then using the GMT birth time of 9.40pm make slight adjustments as follows.

The position of the Sun at noon on 27 July 1941 is 4 degrees 2 minutes Leo. As our subject was born after midday a small amount of time needs to be added on. Applying the same system of adjustment used in chapter 4, (the Sun moving 1 degree per day), we need to add approximately 24 minutes to the Sun's position, thereby making it 4 degrees 26 minutes of Leo. Using the same procedure of adjustment for daily movement as learnt in lesson 4, work out any necessary rectifications for the planets Moon, Mercury, Venus and Mars. Having done so, you should arrive at the following figures:

Sun	4 degrees 26 minutes Leo
Moon	18 degrees Virgo (approximately)
Mercury	15 degrees 03 minutes Virgo
Venus	0 degrees 52 minutes Virgo
Mars	13 degrees 25 minutes Aries

When working out the progressed positions for any other time of the year a few further adjustments are required, mainly to the Moon, which in progression moves approximately one degree per month and takes 2 and a half years to travel through one sign or house. To find the degree of the progressed Moon for any given month in the year, simply add on 1 degree per month from the date of birth, or subtract 1 degree per month for any month prior to the birth. For example, the position of the Moon in December 1963, for our subject will have progressed 5 degrees (August to December) and therefore be at 23 degrees of Virgo. The Moon's position in February 1963, however, would have been 5 degrees less than 18 degrees (March to July) and therefore be at 13 degrees Virgo. Only the Moon requires any major adjustment, but always check the remaining planets to see how fast they are moving, remembering that the daily motion of planets corresponds to a year in progressions. So, for example if Mercury is moving nearly 3 degrees per day, this represents 3 degrees per year.

The Ascendant can also be progressed, and a progressed birth chart erected if desired. To progress the Ascendant use the sidereal time of the new date – in our example case the sidereal time at noon on 27 July 1941, and calculate the new Ascendant in exactly the same manner as for a natal birth chart using the subject's actual birth time. Then place in the planets for the new date using the same system as in chapter 4.

The interpretation of progressed planets is relatively easy. The new positions of the planets are placed on the birth chart (preferably near to the centre of the chart) and then related to the natal chart, noting any change of house or sign, and any new aspects being formed. Due to their very slow movement, however, and the length of time it takes the planets (apart from the Moon) to traverse a few degrees, only a very small orb of 1–2 degrees is allowable for any aspect.

Using our example chart (turn to diagram 3 on page 44) and the calculations for the 21st year as above, we note that progressed Sun at 4 degrees of Leo is situated exactly between (at the midpoint of) Pluto and Venus in Leo, causing a major progression and therefore an important turning-point in the subject's life. Any progressed aspect to Pluto results in transformation, change and the end of an old way of life, whilst progressed aspects

ABOVE YOU'LL NEED AN EPHEMERIS AND BLANK BIRTH CHART TO CALCULATE A PERSON'S PROGRESSIONS AND TRANSITS FOR THE PURPOSES OF PREDICTIVE ASTROLOGY.

to Venus can bring about love, a heightened sense of values and a desire for materialistic security. In our subject's case the two planets are in the sixth house of work and health so the progressed Sun aspect (conjunction) will affect this area of life. A major change of job or place of work could be applicable, with the combining effect of a new, potent love relationship, which may, or may not be the cause of the situation. (Progressed Sun conjunct natal Venus on the Descendant.)

Progressed Moon in the 8th house reaches 19 degrees of Virgo in August (using the 1 degree a month formula) and forms a square to natal Moon in the 11th house, causing possible emotional upsets with friendships and the financial security of loved ones.

Progressed Mercury at 15 degrees of Virgo in the 8th house is not making any aspects, but in 1964 makes a square to natal Moon in the 11th causing further communication problems or challenges with friends or groups situations.

Progressed Venus at 0–1 degree of Virgo is in the 7th house and not forming any aspects.

Progressed Mars at 13 degrees of Aries in the 3rd house is not making any aspects but during 1964 forms a square to the Sun at 14 degrees of Cancer in the 6th house. Arguments or conflicts at work, or health problems relating to the head (Mars in Aries), heart (the Sun) or stomach (the sign Cancer) could arise from this aspect.

GENERAL NOTES ON PROGRESSIONS

- Due to the slowness of movement of progressed planets all aspects must be kept to a maximum 1–2 degree orb.
- Changes of houses or signs occur very infrequently (for example, once every 30 years for the Sun) and are therefore extremely important.
- Progressed planets changing signs can cause subtle changes of character. Thus, a person born with the Sun in Leo will become more earthy and mutable when their progressed Sun enters the sign of Virgo, or somebody born with Mercury in sensitive Cancer

will become more confident in their communication when
progressed Mercury enters the sign of Leo.

- Generally speaking, all the aspects formed by progressed planets
  to natal planets will manifest in a very similar manner to
  natal aspects.

- When a progressed planet enters an empty house it will remain
  in that area for quite some time, thereby helping to bring that area
  to life and creating a tremendous impact on what was once an
  area of disinterest.

- Exact progressed Moon aspects last for approximately one month
  and basically form a monthly cycle of development. Individually
  these aspects seldom create great trauma or action but in
  combination with other major progressions they will act as an
  emotional trigger and intensify the situation.

CALCULATING PROGRESSIONS

In summary therefore, the following formula applies when working
out progressions.

1 Count down in the ephemeris the number of days
   corresponding to the age of the subject.

2 Work across using the GMT lime at birth to calculate in the
   same manner as the natal birth chart, the exact positions of the
   subject's progressed planets (Sun to Mars).

3 Make any necessary adjustments for the time of year in which
   the prediction is taking place, remembering that the movement
   of the planets is correspondingly slowed down, the Sun moving
   1 degree per year. The Moon approximately 12 degrees per
   year, Mercury variable between 0 and 3 degrees per year, Venus
   variable between 0 and 2 degrees per year and Mars rarely
   moving more than 1 degree per year.

TRANSITS

The method of using the daily orbiting transits of the planets in predictive astrology is the easiest and most effective system of all. Quite simply, it entails referring to the ephemeris for any given date in order to find the position of the planets on that day, and then checking to see how they relate to the birth chart.

The five outermost planets, Jupiter to Pluto, are far more important than the personal planets when predicting major events. The personal planets, because of their speed of movement, are better utilized for daily or weekly interpretations on a mundane level.

Using our subject who was born on 6 July 1941, as our example once again, we can turn to any date in any year listed in the ephemeris to find out how the transiting planets will affect his life. To find out what is happening on 6 July 1989 (his 48th birthday) we must turn to the relevant page in the ephemeris for this date and look across at the position of the planets, commencing with the planet Pluto, which is situated at 12 degrees of Scorpio, retrograde, and when placed in the subject's birth chart falls in the otherwise empty 10th house of career, aims and ambitions, adding stimulus and incentive to this area of his life. It does not form any exact major aspects and can therefore be considered to be working on a reasonably positive level.

Moving left across the page we note Neptune's position to be at 10 degrees retrograde of Capricorn, which when placed in our subject's birth chart falls once again in an empty house – this time the 12th. Outer planets transiting the 12th house can sometimes be very problematical, particularly when the house is natally empty. Over-imagination, sacrifices, guilt and secrets can cause depression or unhappiness. When any planets are transiting through the 12th it is an excellent time to take stock of life and endeavour to improve the spiritual qualities, by helping others and sacrificing any excessively materialistic attitudes. Neptune is not making any major aspects and will not do so until it forms an opposition with the Sun in Cancer at

109

14 degrees, in March-April 1990 (check with the ephemeris for these months to see Neptune at 14 degrees of Capricorn).

Moving to the left once more we find Uranus placed at two degrees retrograde of Capricorn and therefore situated in our subject's 11th house of friends and group activities, forming an exact square aspect to Mars at 2 degrees of Aries. Challenges and upsets to the subject's finances and values (2nd house) could therefore occur through unreliable, erratic friends or group situations (Uranus in the 11th).

Saturn is at 10 degrees retrograde of Capricorn, moving down to 9 then 8 degrees by the end of the month. It remains in our subject's 12th house, having entered in the middle of January 1989 (check back in the ephemeris to note this change of house), and makes aspects to both Jupiter (a quincunx) and Mercury (an opposition). The quincunx, in transit, is rarely serious and will only create minor stress in the areas which the two planets occupy. The opposition to Mercury is more forceful and operating from the 12th house of hospitals to the 6th house of health there could well be a spell of health problems or mental depression. Added responsibility or burdens at work (the 6th house) which is an extremely important area for our subject (note the stellium in this house) could also occur.

Transiting Jupiter usually moves fairly quickly and only forms exact aspects for four to five days at a time. On 6 July 1989 it is at 24 degrees of Gemini and therefore placed in our subject's fifth house, hopefully adding benefits within this area – romance, creativity, children, gambling and sports should all prove worthwhile, especially when Jupiter makes good aspects. Looking closely we see that it does in fact form a square to Neptune from approximately 7 to 12 January. Neptune in its negative form indicates escapes and losses and Jupiter when challenged by a square indicates excess, so this brief aspect could predict losses of other people's finances (note that Neptune is situated in the eighth house) or negligent over-optimistic attitudes with children or loved ones.

Judging from the quantity of these challenging aspects, with very few easy ones to mitigate the effect, our subject appears to be going through a difficult spell but if he meets the challenges by relating positively to the planetary energies he will eventually reap the rewards. Negative reactions however will enable the planets to wreak havoc and disruption.

GENERAL NOTES ON TRANSITS

- Planets in transit are much more dynamic and instant in their effect than planets in progression. A transiting planet is extremely powerful when changing from one house to another, especially when moving into an unoccupied house. The sign, however, has much less bearing upon personal lives.

- Due to the retrograde action of the planets some aspects are formed several times within a year (or two, when Pluto is moving at its slowest). The initial forming of the aspect is usually the most powerful, but sometimes the very last return of the aspect can be the most crucial.

- The transiting energy of the, planets is very similar to that projected in the natal charts. For example, Pluto will cause volcanic eruption, transformation and trauma, and Neptune will create confusion, chaos, misunderstanding, losses etc.

- When looking at the personal planets, the current position of Mars will signify the area in which much of the present energy is being expended. Venus will denote an area of temporary harmony and peace. Mercury shows the area in which communication is likely to occur and the Sun provides ego, strength and a sense of purpose to whichever house it is occupying.

- Conjunctions are the most potent of transiting aspects, their effect being twice as strong as a square, opposition or trine.

- Some people do not respond very noticeably to any transiting aspects, whereas others respond to the slightest stimulus

- The hypothesis that any planet can operate negatively or positively within a birth chart, also applies to transits, but it can

111

be very difficult to harness the potent energy of the three outermost planets, Uranus, Neptune and Pluto, especially if they are aspected in a difficult way within the birth chart.

- Transiting aspects can manifest in a multitude of ways, and it is not easy to pinpoint exactly what will happen to a subject – one can only outline several indications of direction. Thus Uranus transiting the fifth house could encourage sudden, exciting romantic affairs, or induce children to behave rebelliously. It could also give tremendous potential for startling, exciting creative activity. It may even spur the subject into taking up a new hobby such as flying or computer studies (both ruled by Uranus).

MAJOR PLANETARY CYCLES

Planets vary in the length of time it takes them to travel through the birth chart and form their own cycles:

PLUTO

Because Pluto moves extremely slowly and somewhat erratically, taking between 10 and 30 years to travel through one sign or house, it is impossible for any person to experience a complete cycle of this tiny planet. It may only transit two or three signs or houses within a lifetime. Therefore, the movement of Pluto from one house into another signifies a vitally transforming period of life. The aspects Pluto forms whilst in transit must always be observed carefully as no other planet is capable of causing quite so much trauma when operating negatively.

NEPTUNE

Neptune, too, moves very slowly (changing signs approximately once every 14 years) and will seldom, therefore, move more than

ABOVE WHEN PLUTO CHANGES HOUSE (JUST TWO OR THREE TIMES IN A LIFETIME) ITS INFLUENCE IS STRONG.

five or six signs or houses throughout a lifetime. The major aspect Neptune forms during its long cycle is the square to natal Neptune, which occurs during the early to middle forties and coincides with the mid-life crisis. It can often be a confusing, disorientating time with a desire for a change of direction in life.

URANUS

The Uranus cycle is speedier (seven years to transit a sign or house). It is possible to experience this planet's return to its natal (birth) position, at around the age of 84. This cycle is called a Uranus Return. Many people who survive to the age of 84 experience a most unexpected new lease of life at this time. The second, if not the most important event in the Uranus cycle is the Uranus half return (when Uranus opposes its natal birth position), which occurs anytime between the late 30s and early 40s. This aspect, too, coincides with the onset of middle age and often causes much disruption, rebellion and search for independence. Women especially feel the urge to be free and seek out drastic changes within their previously secure lives. It is very much a time for coming to terms with one's own needs and creative outlets. Uranus square Uranus, which occurs between the ages of 19 and 21, is a similar period of seeking one's own identity and freedom.

SATURN

Saturn's cycle is much faster – it takes only 2 and a half years for this planet to travel through one sign or house, and therefore 28 to 30 years for it to reach the same position it occupied at birth (the first Saturn Return). Between the ages of 56 and 58 Saturn returns for the second time, and for a third time (if you are lucky) at approximately 87. The first Saturn return is regarded as the most significant, and its effects are extremely diverse, applying to almost anything from a broken marriage, a birth of a child, a severe period of depression or a profound spell of creativity. Marriages, too, are extremely common during this time.

Saturn is regarded as a teacher, and if we learn our lessons well we are duly rewarded. There are some people, however, who make the same mistakes over and over again, and these people often have Saturn dominant in their chart. They appear to be afraid of moving in the right direction, of taking chances in life and giving up their strong material instincts. If the required lessons have not been learnt by the end of the first Saturn Return, the second can be equally traumatic.

JUPITER

Jupiter takes approximately 1 year to travel through 1 sign or house and 12 years to complete its cycle. The first Jupiter return at around the age of 12 marks a turning point in one's physical development, the second, at approximately 24, in one's emotional development, and the third, at 36, in one's active development. The fourth, at the age of 48, heralds the onset of middle age. Each 12-year cycle indicates a major expansion in one's life and is usually an important, uplifting time.

ABOVE JUPITER'S EFFECT IS STRONGEST WHEN RETURNING TO THE POSITION IT OCCUPIED AT BIRTH IN COMPLETION OF ITS 12-YEAR CYCLE.

SUN, MOON, MERCURY, VENUS AND MARS

All these planets have important cycles, the Sun 30 days, (and 1 year), the Moon 28 days, Mercury, Venus and Mars variable, which are influential on a day to day basis, but nowhere so intense in their effect as the outer planets.

APPENDICES

APPENDIX 1: BRITISH SUMMERTIME 1916 TO 2000

	COMMENCED	ENDED
1916	21 MAY	1 OCT.
1917	8 APR.	17 SEPT.
1918	24 MAR.	30 SEPT.
1919	30 MAR.	29 SEPT.
1920	28 MAR.	25 OCT.
1921	3 APR.	3 OCT.
1922	26 MAR.	8 OCT.
1923	22 APR.	16 SEPT.
1924	20 APR.	21 SEPT.
1925 TO	3RD SUN. IN	1 SUN. IN
1938 INCL.	APR.	OCT.
1939	16 APR.	19 NOV.
1940	25 FEB.	CONTINUED

1941-4 INCL. CONTINUATION OF BRITISH SUMMERTIME THROUGHOUT THESE YEARS, PLUS THE ADDITION OF DOUBLE SUMMERTIME.

	COMMENCED	ENDED
1941	4 MAY	10 AUG.
1942	5 APR.	9 AUG.
1943	4 APR.	15 AUG.
1944	2 APR.	17 SEPT.
1945	2 APR.	15 JULY.
1945	CONTINUED	7 OCT.
1946	14 APR.	6 OCT.
1947	16 APR.	2 NOV.

PLUS DOUBLE SUMMERTIME BETWEEN

	COMMENCED	ENDED
1947	13 APR.	10 AUG.

	COMMENCED	ENDED
1948	14 MAR.	31 OCT.
1949	3 APR.	30 OCT.
1950	16 APR.	22 OCT.
1951	15 APR.	21 OCT.
1952	20 APR.	26 OCT.
1953	19 APR.	4 OCT.
1954	11 APR.	3 OCT.
1955	17 APR.	2 OCT.
1956	15 APR.	7 OCT.
1957	14 APR.	6 OCT.
1958	20 APR.	5 OCT.
1959	19 APR.	4 OCT.
1960	10 APR.	2 OCT.
1961	26 MAR.	29 OCT.
1962	25 MAR.	28 OCT.
1963	31 MAR.	27 OCT.
1964	22 MAR.	25 OCT.
1965	21 MAR.	24 OCT.
1966	20 MAR.	23 OCT.
1967	19 MAR.	29 OCT.
1968 TO	18 FEB.	CONTINUED
1970 INCL.	CONTINUED WITH BRITISH SUMMERTIME	
1971	CONTINUED	31 OCT.
1972	19 MAR.	28 OCT.
1973	18 MAR.	28 OCT.
1974	17 MAR.	27 OCT.

	COMMENCED	ENDED
1975	16 MAR.	26 OCT.
1976	21 MAR.	24 OCT.
1977	20 MAR.	23 OCT.
1978	19 MAR.	29 OCT.
1979	18 MAR.	28 OCT.
1980	16 MAR.	26 OCT.
1981	29 MAR.	25 OCT.
1982	28 MAR.	24 OCT.
1983	27 MAR.	23 OCT.
1984	25 MAR.	28 OCT.
1985	31 MAR.	27 OCT.
1986	30 MAR.	26 OCT.
1987	29 MAR.	25 OCT.
1988	27 MAR.	23 OCT.
1989	26 MAR.	29 OCT.
1990	25 MAR.	28 OCT.
1991	31 MAR.	27 OCT.
1992	29 MAR.	25 OCT.
1993	28 MAR.	31 OCT.
1994	27 MAR.	30 OCT.
1995	26 MAR.	29 OCT.
1996	31 MAR.	27 OCT.
1997	30 MAR.	26 OCT.
1998	29 MAR.	28 OCT.
1999	28 MAR.	31 OCT.
2000	26 MAR.	29 OCT.

NOTE: ALL TIMES CHANGE AT 2.00 AM GMT

APPENDIX 2: POSITIONS OF PLUTO

1941

1/1	3	40	R
1/2	2	59	R
15/4	2	01	DD
24/6	3	01	D
30/7	4	00	D
6/9	5	00	D
7/11	5	47	RR
31/12	5	10	R

1963

1/1	12	04	R
9/1	11	59	R
25/2	10	59	R
7/4	9	59	R
24/5	9	32	DD
4/7	10	01	D
9/8	11	00	D
8/9	12	01	D
7/10	13	00	D
18/11	14	00	D
18/12	14	13	RR
31/12	14	10	R

1970

1/1	27	23	R
7/2	26	58	R
19/3	25	59	R
30/4	24	59	R
6/6	24	40	DD
10/7	25	00	D
17/8	26	00	D
14/9	27	00	D
12/10	28	02	D
12/11	29	00	D
31/12	29	42	D

KEY R – RETROGRADE D – DIRECT RR – TURNED RETROGRADE ON GIVEN DATE DD – TURNED DIRECT ON GIVEN DATE

115

New Moon – July 24, 7h 88m 40s am

14					JULY, 1941.				[R A P H A E L'S

D M	Neptune Lat.	Dec.	Herschel Lat.	Dec.	Saturn Lat.	Dec.	Jupiter Lat.	Dec.	Mars Lat.	Declin.
1	1 N 16	3 N 7	0 S 13	19 N 39	2 S 4	16 N 53	0 S 41	21 N 0	3 S 14	3 S 8 · 2 S 55
3	1 16	3 6	0 13	19 40	2 4	16 56	0 41	21 4	3 17	2 43 · 2 31
5	1 16	3 5	0 13	19 41	2 4	16 59	0 41	21 8	3 20	2 19 · 2 7
7	1 16	3 4	0 13	19 43	2 4	17 1	0 41	21 12	3 23	1 55 · 1 43
9	1 16	3 4	0 13	19 44	2 5	17 4	0 41	21 16	3 27	1 31 · 1 20
11	1 16	3 3	0 13	19 45	2 5	17 6	0 41	21 20	3 30	1 8 · 0 57
13	1 15	3 2	0 13	19 46	2 5	17 9	0 41	21 23	3 33	0 45 · 0 34
15	1 15	3 1	0 13	19 47	2 5	17 11	0 41	21 27	3 36	0 23 · 0 12
17	1 15	3 0	0 13	19 48	2 6	17 13	0 41	21 30	3 39	0 2 · 0 N 9
19	1 15	2 59	0 13	19 49	2 6	17 15	0 41	21 33	3 42	0 N.19 · 0 30
21	1 15	2 57	0 13	19 50	2 6	17 17	0 41	21 36	3 45	0 40 · 0 50
23	1 15	2 56	0 13	19 51	2 6	17 19	0 41	21 39	3 48	1 0 · 1 9
25	1 15	2 55	0 13	19 52	2 7	17 21	0 41	21 42	3 51	1 19 · 1 28
27	1 15	2 54	0 13	19 52	2 7	17 23	0 41	21 45	3 54	1 38 · 1 47
29	1 15	2 53	0 13	19 53	2 7	17 24	0 41	21 48	3 57	1 56 · 2 4
31	1 15	2 51	0 13	19 54	2 8	17 26	0 41	21 50	4 0	2 13

D M	D W	Sidereal Time H. M. S.	☉ Long.	☉ Dec.	☽ Long.	☽ Lat.	☽ Dec.	MIDNIGHT. ☽ Long.	☽ Dec.
1	Tu	6 36 35	9♋14 20	23 N 7	0♎24 46	0 N24	0 N12	7♎20 11	1 S 59
2	W	6 40 32	10 11 32	23 3	14 19 18	1 36	4 S 10	21 22 7	6 19
3	Th	6 44 29	11 8 44	22 59	28 28 34	2 44	8 23	5♏38 29	10 21
4	F	6 48 25	12 5 56	22 54	12♏51 34	3 42	12 10	20 7 26	13 49
5	S	6 52 22	13 3 7	22 48	27 25 30	4 26	15 16	4♐45 8	16 28
6	☉	6 56 18	14 0 18	22 43	12♐5 31	4 54	17 23	19 25 48	18 2
7	M	7 0 15	14 57 29	22 36	26 45 2	5 2	18 22	4♑2 16	18 24
8	Tu	7 4 11	15 54 40	22 30	11♑16 35	4 51	18 8	18 27 6	17 35
9	W	7 8 8	16 51 51	22 23	25 33 4	4 21	16 45	2≈33 49	15 41
10	Th	7 12 5	17 49 2	22 16	9≈28 51	3 37	14 24	16 17 51	12 56
11	F	7 16 1	18 46 13	22 8	23 0 38	2 41	11 19	29 37 9	9 35
12	S	7 19 58	19 43 25	22 0	6♓33 1	38	7 45	12♓32 3	5 51
13	☉	7 23 54	20 40 38	21 51	18 51 2	0 32	3 56	25 4 56	1 59
14	M	7 27 51	21 37 51	21 42	1♈14 18	0 S 34	0 2	7♈19 41	1 N 53
15	Tu	7 31 47	22 35 4	21 33	13 21 43	1 38	3 N 47	19 21 3	5 37
16	W	7 35 44	23 32 18	21 24	25 13 20	2 36	7 22	1♉14 15	9 4
17	Th	7 39 40	24 29 33	21 14	7♉8 9	3 26	10 39	13 4 31	12 8
18	F	7 43 37	25 26 49	21 3	19 0 7	4 8	13 29	24 56 48	14 43
19	S	7 47 33	26 24 5	20 53	0♊55 6	4 40	15 47	6♊55 30	16 41
20	☉	7 51 30	27 21 22	20 42	12 58 25	4 59	17 25	19 4 13	17 57
21	M	7 55 27	28 18 39	20 30	25 13 13	5 18	17	1♋25 37	18 23
22	Tu	7 59 23	29 15 57	20 19	7♋41 37	4 57	18 17	14 1 17	17 57
23	W	8 3 20	0♌13 16	20 6	20 24 40	4 34	17 23	26 51 44	16 35
24	Th	8 7 11	1 10 36	19 54	3♌22 23	3 57	15 34	9♌56 32	14 20
25	F	8 11 13	2 7 56	19 41	16 33 59	3 6	12 55	23 14 35	11 19
26	S	8 15 9	3 5 17	19 28	29 58 7	2 4	9 33	6♍44 26	7 39
27	☉	8 19 6	4 2 38	19 15	13♍33 20	0 54	5 38	20 24 39	3 32
28	M	8 23 2	5 0 0	19 1	27 18 14	0 N20	1 22	4♎13 58	0 S 49
29	Tu	8 26 59	5 57 23	18 47	11♎11 44	1 33	3 S 0	18 11 24	5 9
30	W	8 30 56	6 54 46	18 33	25 12 53	2 42	7 15	2♏16 2	9 14
31	Th	8 34 52	7 52 9	18 18	9♏20 44	3 41	11 7	16 26 47	12 49

First Quarter – July 2, 4h 23m 59s am; July 31, 9h 19m 10s am

New Moon – July 8, 8*h* 17*m* 20*s* *am*

EPHEMERIS] **JULY, 1941.** 15

D M	Venus. Lat. ° ′	Venus. Declin. ° ′	Venus. Declin. ° ′	Mercury. Lat. ° ′	Mercury. Declin. ° ′	Mercury. Declin. ° ′	☽ Node. ° ′
1	1 N 27	21 N 50		4 S 20	18 N 39		26 ♍ 34
			21 N 36			18 N 33	
3	1 29	21 21		4 36	18 28		26 27
			21 5			18 25	
5	1 31	20 49		4 44	18 23		26 21
			20 32			18 22	
7	1 32	20 15		4 50	18 23		26 15
			19 57			18 25	
9	1 33	19 38		4 47	18 28		26 8
			19 20			18 33	
11	1 34	19 0		4 39	18 38		26 2
			18 40			18 45	
13	1 35	18 20		4 25	18 53		25 56
			17 59			19 2	
15	1 36	17 37		4 7	19 11		25 49
			17 15			19 21	
17	1 36	16 53		3 45	19 32		25 43
			16 30			19 43	
19	1 35	16 7		3 20	19 54		25 36
			15 43			20 5	
21	1 35	15 19		2 52	20 17		25 30
			14 54			20 28	
23	1 34	14 29		2 24	20 39		25 24
			14 4			20 49	
25	1 33	13 38		1 54	20 58		25 17
			13 12			21 7	
27	1 32	12 46		1 25	21 14		25 11
			12 19			21 20	
29	1 30	11 52		0 56	21 25		25 5
			11 25			21 28	
31	1 28	10 58		0 28	21 29		24 58

Mutual Aspects.

1. ☉∠♄. ♀✱♅. ♂P♆.
2. ☉☌☿. ♀△♂.
4. ☿∠♄. ♀P♃.
5. ☉Q♆. ☿⊻♃. ♀☌♇.
6. ☉∠♅.
8. ☉⊥♃. ☿⊻♀. ♀Q♄. ♂△♇. ♄△♆.
9. ♀P♅.
10. ♀✱♃, ∠♆. 11. ♀Q♅.
12. ☿⊥ & P♀.
13. ☿□♂.
16. ☉P♃. ♀P♄.
18. ☉✱♆. ♀⊥♆.
19. ☉✱♄. ☿P♅.
20. ☉∠♃.
22. ☉P☿, ✱♅. ♀Q♃.
23. ☿∠♀. ♀⊻♆. ♂∠♄.
24. ☉P♅. ☿∠♄. ♀⚼♂, □♄.
25. ☿□♂.
26. ☿⊻♃, Q♆. ♀□♅.
27. ☉☌♇. ☿∠♅.
28. ♂✱♃. 30. ♀⊻♇.
31. ☿∠♀, ⊥♃. ♂∠♅.

D M	♆ Long. ° ′	♅ Long. ° ′	♄ Long. ° ′	♃ Long. ° ′	♂ Long. ° ′	♀ Long. ° ′	☿ Long. ° ′	☉	♇	♆	♅	♄	♃	♂	♀	☿
1	25 ♍ 5	28 ♉ 39	24 ♉ 28	8 ♊ 13	29 ♓ 35	28 ♋ 46	11 ♋ 24		✱	☌	△	△		☍	✱	
2	25 6	28 42	24 34	8 26	0 ♈ 10	29 59	10 ℞ 47	□			⚼	⚼	△			□
3	25 7	28 45	24 40	8 39	0 45	1 ♌ 12	10 11		□	⊻			⚼		□	
4	25 8	28 47	24 46	8 52	1 19	2 25	9 35	△		∠				⚼		△
5	25 9	28 50	24 52	9 5	1 53	3 39	9 1	⚼	△	✱	☍	☍		△	△	⚼
𝕾	25 10	28 53	24 58	9 18	2 27	4 52	8 28		⚼				☍			
7	25 11	28 55	25 4	9 30	3 1	6 5	7 58			□				□	⚼	
8	25 12	28 58	25 10	9 43	3 34	7 18	7 31	☍			⚼	⚼				☍
9	25 13	29 1	25 16	9 56	4 8	8 31	7 8			△	△	△	⚼			
10	25 14	29 3	25 21	10 8	4 41	9 44	6 49		☍	⚼			△	✱	☍	
11	25 15	29 6	25 27	10 21	5 13	10 57	6 34				□	□		∠		⚼
12	25 16	29 8	25 33	10 33	5 46	12 10	6 23	⚼					□	⊻		△
𝕾	25 17	29 11	25 38	10 45	6 18	13 23	6 18	△	⚼							
14	25 18	29 13	25 44	10 58	6 50	14 36	6 D 18		△	☍	✱	✱		☌	⚼	□
15	25 20	29 16	25 49	11 10	7 21	15 50	6 23				∠	∠	✱		△	
16	25 21	29 18	25 54	11 22	7 53	17 3	6 33	□			⊻	⊻	∠			
17	25 22	29 20	26 0	11 34	8 24	18 16	6 49		□	⚼			⊻	⊻		✱
18	25 23	29 23	26 5	11 46	8 54	19 28	7 11							∠	□	∠
19	25 25	29 25	26 10	11 58	9 25	20 41	7 38	✱	✱	△	☌	☌				
𝕾	25 26	29 27	26 15	12 10	9 55	21 54	8 11	∠	∠				☌	✱		⊻
21	25 28	29 29	26 20	12 22	10 24	23 7	8 50	⊻		□	⊻	⊻			✱	
22	25 29	29 31	26 25	12 33	10 53	24 20	9 34		⊻			∠	⊻	□	∠	☌
23	25 30	29 33	26 30	12 45	11 22	25 33	10 23			✱	∠	✱			⊻	
24	25 32	29 36	26 34	12 56	11 51	26 46	11 18	☌	☌		✱		∠			
25	25 33	29 38	26 39	13 8	12 19	27 59	12 18			∠			✱	△		⊻
26	25 35	29 40	26 44	13 19	12 47	29 12	13 24	⊻	⊻	⊻	□	□		⚼	☌	∠
𝕾	25 36	29 41	26 48	13 30	13 14	0 ♍ 24	14 34	∠	∠				□			✱
28	25 38	29 43	26 52	13 42	13 41	1 37	15 50		✱	☌	△	△			⊻	
29	25 39	29 45	26 57	13 53	14 7	2 50	17 11	✱			⚼	⚼	△	☍		□
30	25 41	29 47	27 1	14 4	14 33	4 3	18 36			⊻			⚼		∠	
31	25 43	29 49	27 5	14 15	14 59	5 15	20 6	□	□	∠					✱	

Last Quarter – July 16, 8*h* 7*m* 19*s* *am*

New Moon – October 17, 0h 43m pm

20						OCTOBER, 1963					[RAPHAEL'S		
D	Neptune.		Herschel.		Saturn.		Jupiter.		Mars.				
M	Lat.	Dec.	Lat.	Dec.	Lat.	Dec.	Lat.	Dec.	Lat.	Dec.			
1	1 N43	14 S 25	0 N44	9 N23	1 S 15	17 S 0	1 S 38	4 N33	0 S 21	16 S 4	16 S 17
3	1 43	14 26	0 44	9 20	1 15	17 1	1 38	4 27	0 22	16 30	16 43
5	1 43	14 27	0 44	9 18	1 15	17 2	1 38	4 21	0 24	16 56	17 8
7	1 43	14 28	0 44	9 15	1 15	17 3	1 38	4 14	0 25	17 21	17 33
9	1 43	14 29	0 44	9 13	1 15	17 4	1 38	4 8	0 26	17 45	17 57
11	1 43	14 31	0 44	9 11	1 15	17 4	1 38	4 2	0 27	18 9	18 21
13	1 43	14 32	0 44	9 8	1 15	17 5	1 38	3 56	0 29	18 33	18 45
15	1 43	14 33	0 44	9 6	1 14	17 5	1 38	3 50	0 30	18 56	19 7
17	1 43	14 35	0 44	9 4	1 14	17 5	1 37	3 44	0 31	19 18	19 29
19	1 43	14 36	0 44	9 2	1 14	17 5	1 37	3 38	0 32	19 40	19 51
21	1 43	14 37	0 44	9 0	1 14	17 5	1 37	3 32	0 33	20 1	20 12
23	1 43	14 38	0 44	8 58	1 14	17 5	1 37	3 27	0 34	20 22	20 32
25	1 43	14 40	0 45	8 56	1 14	17 5	1 36	3 21	0 35	20 42	20 51
27	1 43	14 41	0 45	8 54	1 14	17 5	1 36	3 16	0 36	21 1	21 10
29	1 43	14 42	0 45	8 52	1 14	17 4	1 36	3 11	0 38	21 19	21 28
31	1 43	14 44	0 45	8 51	1 14	17 3	1 35	3 6	0 39	21 37	

D	D	Sidereal	☉	☉	☽	☽	☽	MIDNIGHT	
M	W	Time.	Long.	Dec.	Long.	Lat.	Dec.	☽Long.	☽Dec.
		H. M. S.							
1	Tu	12 38 0	7≏35 11	3 S 1	14♓17 48	4 S 14	10 S 5	21♓32 42	7 S 31
2	W	12 41 56	8 34 10	3 24	28 53 13	4 46	4 49	6♈18 24	2 1
3	Th	12 45 53	9 33 12	3 47	13♈47 13	5 0	0 N 50	21 18 26	3 N 41
4	F	12 49 49	10 32 15	4 10	28 50 47	4 53	6 29	6♉23 1	9 12
5	S	12 53 46	11 31 21	4 34	13♉53 52	4 26	11 46	21 22 14	14 9
6	☉	12 57 43	12 30 29	4 57	28 47 8	3 42	16 17	6♊7 46	18 9
7	M	13 1 39	13 29 39	5 20	13♊23 31	2 43	19 43	20 33 59	20 57
8	Tu	13 5 36	14 28 51	5 43	27 38 55	1 35	21 35	4♋38 15	22 22
9	W	13 9 32	15 28 6	6 6	11♋32 2	0 23	22 33	18 20 27	22 24
10	Th	13 13 29	16 27 24	6 28	25 3 45	0 N 48	21 55	1♌42 13	21 7
11	F	13 17 25	17 26 43	6 51	8♌16 14	1 55	20 3	14 46 7	18 44
12	S	13 21 22	18 26 5	7 14	21 12 13	2 54	17 11	27 34 53	15 27
13	☉	13 25 18	19 25 29	7 36	3♍54 25	3 44	13 33	10♍11 5	11 31
14	M	13 29 15	20 24 56	7 59	16 25 6	4 22	9 23	22 36 43	7 10
15	Tu	13 33 12	21 24 24	8 21	28 46 4	4 47	4 53	4≏53 18	2 34
16	W	13 37 8	22 23 55	8 43	10≏58 34	4 59	0 14	17 1 58	2 S 5
17	Th	13 41 5	23 23 28	9 5	23 3 36	4 57	4 S 22	29 3 37	6 36
18	F	13 45 1	24 23 2	9 27	5♏ 2 7	4 42	8 47	10♏59 17	10 51
19	S	13 48 58	25 22 39	9 49	16 55 18	4 12	12 50	22 50 23	14 41
20	☉	13 52 54	26 22 18	10 11	28 44 48	3 36	16 23	4♐38 54	17 55
21	M	13 56 51	27 21 58	10 32	10♐33 1	2 48	19 16	16 27 34	20 25
22	Tu	14 0 47	28 21 41	10 54	22 23 2	1 53	21 21	28 19 56	22 3
23	W	14 4 44	29 21 25	11 15	4♑18 49	0 52	22 30	10♑15 20	17 42
24	Th	14 8 41	0♏21 11	11 36	16 24 58	0 S 12	22 38	22 33 30	22 17
25	F	14 12 37	1 20 59	11 57	28 46 34	1 17	21 40	5♒ 4 48	20 46
26	S	14 16 34	2 20 48	12 17	11♒28 50	2 20	19 35	17 59 16	18 8
27	☉	14 20 30	3 20 39	12 38	24 36 34	3 18	16 25	1♓21 11	14 28
28	M	14 24 27	4 20 32	12 58	8♓13 21	4 6	12 17	15 13 12	9 55
29	Tu	14 28 23	5 20 26	13 18	22 38 48	5 1	1 51	29 35 21	4 39
30	W	14 32 20	6 20 22	13 38	6♈56 48	5 1	1 N 55	14♈24 13	1 N 1
31	Th	14 36 16	7 20 20	13 58	21 56 36	5 0	3 N 55	29 32 45	6 46

First Quarter – October 25, 5h 21m pm

New Moon – October 3, 4*h* 44*m* 40*s am*

EPHEMERIS] **OCTOBER, 1963** 21

D M	Venus Lat. ° ′	Venus Declin. ° ′	Venus Declin. ° ′	Mercury Lat. ° ′	Mercury Declin. ° ′	Mercury Declin. ° ′	☽ Node. ° ′
1	1N 4	5 S 25	5 S 55	0N 29	4 N 2	4 N 5	16♋12
3	1 1	6 25	6 55	0 57	4 3	3 56	16 6
5	0 58	7 25	7 54	1 20	3 45	3 29	16 0
7	0 54	8 23	8 53	1 37	3 10	2 46	15 53
9	0 50	9 22	9 50	1 49	2 20	1 50	15 47
11	0 46	10 19	10 47	1 56	1 18	0 44	15 41
13	0 42	11 15	11 43	1 59	0 8	0 S 30	15 34
15	0 38	12 10	12 37	1 58	1 S 9	1 50	15 28
17	0 34	13 4	13 31	1 55	2 31	3 13	15 21
19	0 29	13 57	14 23	1 49	3 55	4 38	15 15
21	0 24	14 49	15 14	1 41	5 21	6 4	15 9
23	0 20	15 39	16 3	1 31	6 47	7 30	15 2
25	0 15	16 27	16 51	1 21	8 12	8 54	14 56
27	0 10	17 14	17 37	1 9	9 36	10 18	14 50
29	0 5	17 59	18 21	0 57	10 59	11 39	14 43
31	0 0	18 42		0 44	12 19		14 37

Mutual Aspects.

1. ☉⊻♅, ⊥♆. ♀△♄.
3. ♀⊥♇. ♂☌♆. [♂⚹♇
4. ☉P☿. ☿±♄. ♂∇♃.
5. ☉P♃.
6. ☉⊻♇. ♀∠♅. ♂□♄,
8. ☉☍♃, ⊥♅, ⊻♆. [P♄.
9. ♀P♅. ♃∇♆.
10. ☉△♄. ☿∠♆. ♀∠♇. ♃±♅.
11. ☿⚼♄. ♂±♃. ♂Q♅.
13. ☉⊥♇. 15. ☿∠♂. ♂P♇.
16. ☿⊻♅, ⊥♆.
17. ☉∠♅, P♅. ♃∇♇.
18. ☿☍♃, ⊻♇.
19. ☿P♃, ⊥♅, ⊻♆. ♀⚹♅.
20. ☉⊻♂. ☿△♄. [♂Q♇.
21. ♀P♆. ♄Stat.
22. ☉∠♇. ☿⊥♇. ♀∇♃. ♂⚼♃.
23. ♀⚹♇. 24. ☿⊥♂. ♀☌♆.
25. ☿∠♅. ♀□♄.
26. ☿P♅. ♀±♃.
27. ☿∠♇. ♀P♄.
29. ♀Q♅. 31. ☿⊻♂. ♀P♇.

D M	♆ Long. ° ′	♅ Long. ° ′	♄ Long. ° ′	♃ Long. ° ′	♂ Long. ° ′	♀ Long. ° ′	☿ Long. ° ′	☉	♇	♆	♅	♄	♃	♂	♀	☿
								Lunar Aspects.								
1	14♏ 3	7♍40	16♒47	15♈22	12♏58	16≏19	20♍57		☍	△	☍	⊻	⊻	△		☍
2	14 5	7 43	16 ℞45	15 ℞14	13 39	17 34	21 24			⚼		∠		⚼		
3	14 7	7 46	16 43	15 6	14 21	18 48	22 0	☍				⚹	☌		☍	
4	14 9	7 50	16 42	14 58	15 2	20 3	22 45		⚼		⚼					
5	14 11	7 53	16 40	14 50	15 44	21 18	23 38		△	☍	△	□	⊻	☍		⚼
S	14 13	7 56	16 38	14 42	16 26	22 33	24 39	⚼					∠			△
7	14 15	7 59	16 37	14 34	17 7	23 47	25 47	△	□		□	△	⚹		⚼	
8	14 17	8 3	16 36	14 26	17 49	25 2	27 1			⚼		⚼		⚼	△	□
9	14 19	8 6	16 34	14 18	18 31	26 17	28 20	□	⚹	△	⚹		□			
10	14 21	8 9	16 33	14 10	19 13	27 32	29 44		∠		∠			△	□	⚹
11	14 23	8 12	16 32	14 2	19 55	28 46	1≏11		⊻	□	⊻		△			
12	14 25	8 15	16 31	13 54	20 37	0♏ 1	2 42	⚹				☍		□		∠
S	14 27	8 18	16 30	13 46	21 19	1 16	4 16	∠			☌		⚼		⚹	⊻
14	14 29	8 21	16 29	13 38	22 2	2 31	5 52	⊻	☌	⚹				⚹	∠	
15	14 31	8 24	16 29	13 30	22 44	3 46	7 29			∠		⚼			⊻	
16	14 33	8 27	16 28	13 22	23 26	5 0	9 8		⊻	⊻	⊻	△	☍	∠		☌
17	14 35	8 30	16 28	13 14	24 9	6 15	10 49	☌	∠		∠			⊻		
18	14 37	8 33	16 27	13 6	24 51	7 30	12 30				⚹				☌	
19	14 40	8 36	16 27	12 58	25 34	8 45	14 12		⚹	☌		□				⊻
S	14 42	8 39	16 27	12 51	26 16	10 0	15 54	⊻					⚼	☌		∠
21	14 44	8 42	16 27	12 43	26 59	11 14	17 36	∠	□	⊻	□	⚹	△		⊻	
22	14 46	8 44	16 D27	12 36	27 42	12 29	19 18							⊻	∠	⚹
23	14 48	8 47	16 27	12 28	28 25	13 44	21 0	⚹		∠	△	∠				
24	14 50	8 50	16 27	12 21	29 8	14 59	22 42		△	⚹		⊻	□	∠	⚹	
25	14 53	8 52	16 28	12 14	29 51	16 14	24 24	□	⚼		⚼			⚹		□
26	14 55	8 55	16 28	12 7	0♐34	17 28	26 6			□		☌	⚹			
S	14 57	8 58	16 29	12 0	1 17	18 43	27 47						∠		□	△
28	14 59	9 0	16 29	11 53	2 0	19 58	29 28	△	☍	△	☍		⊻	□		
29	15 1	9 3	16 30	11 46	2 43	21 13	1♏ 8	⚼				⊻			△	⚼
30	15 4	9 5	16 31	11 39	3 27	22 28	2 48			⚼		∠	☌	△	⚼	
31	15 6	9 8	16 32	11 33	4 10	23 42	4 27		⚼		⚼	⚹		⚼		

Last Quarter – October 9, 7*h* 28*m pm*

New Moon – February 23, 9h 13m pm (4° ♓ 56')

4			FEBRUARY, 1982					[RAPHAEL'S
D	D	Sidereal	☉	☉	☽	☽	☽	☽	MIDNIGHT
M	W	Time	Long.	Dec.	Long.	Lat.	Dec.	Node	☽ Long.	☽ Dec.

D M	D W	Sidereal Time H. M. S.	☉ Long. ° ′ ″	☉ Dec. ° ′	☽ Long. ° ′ ″	☽ Lat. ° ′	☽ Dec. ° ′	☽ Node ° ′	☽ Long. ° ′	☽ Dec. ° ′
1	M	20 45 28	12≈18 16	17S 7	10♉57 52	4S 59	10N22	21♋31	17♉59 0	12N38
2	Tu	20 49 24	13 19 9	16 49	25 3 12	4 26	14 44	21 28	2Ⅱ10 17	16 38
3	W	20 53 21	14 20 0	16 32	9Ⅱ20 0	3 36	18 18	21 25	16 32 1	19 42
4	Th	20 57 17	15 20 50	16 14	23 45 57	2 31	20 47	21 22	1♋ 1	21 31
5	F	21 1 14	16 21 39	15 56	8♋17 38	1S 17	21 54	21 18	15 34 14	21 55
6	S	21 5 11	17 22 26	15 38	22 50 26	0N 3	21 33	21 15	0♌ 5 33	20 49
7	☉	21 9 7	18 23 12	15 19	7♌18 50	1 21	19 45	21 12	14 29 34	18 22
8	M	21 13 4	19 23 57	15 0	21 37 2	2 34	16 43	21 9	28 40 37	14 51
9	Tu	21 17 0	20 24 40	14 41	5♍39 42	3 36	12 46	21 6	12♍33 51	10 33
10	W	21 20 57	21 25 22	14 22	19 22 40	4 23	8 14	21 3	26 5 54	5 51
11	Th	21 24 53	22 26 3	14 2	2≏43 26	4 55	3 N26	20 59	9≏15 17	1 N 0
12	F	21 28 50	23 26 42	13 42	15 41 31	5 11	1 S 24	20 56	22 2 24	3 S 45
13	S	21 32 46	24 27 21	13 22	28 18 13	5 11	6 2	20 53	4♏29 24	8 13
14	☉	21 36 43	25 27 58	13 2	10♏36 24	4 56	10 19	20 50	16 39 46	12 17
15	M	21 40 40	26 28 34	12 41	22 40 5	4 29	14 6	20 47	28 37 56	15 47
16	Tu	21 44 36	27 29 9	12 21	4♐33 33	3 50	17 20	20 44	10♐28 51	18 36
17	W	21 48 33	28 29 43	12 0	16 23 12	3 2	19 44	20 40	22 17 39	20 38
18	Th	21 52 29	29≈30 15	11 39	28 12 51	2 6	21 20	20 37	4♑ 9 23	21 47
19	F	21 56 26	0♓30 47	11 18	10♑ 7 50	1 N 4	21 59	20 34	16 8 42	21 56
20	S	22 0 22	1 31 17	10 56	22 12 28	0S 12	21 38	20 31	28 19 33	21 4
21	☉	22 4 19	2 31 45	10 34	4≈30 19	1 8	20 14	20 28	10≈45 3	19 9
22	M	22 8 15	3 32 12	10 13	17 3 58	2 12	17 49	20 24	23 27 10	16 15
23	Tu	22 12 12	4 32 37	9 51	29 54 44	3 11	14 29	20 21	6♓26 37	12 30
24	W	22 16 8	5 33 1	9 29	13♓ 2 42	4 1	10 22	20 18	19 42 48	8 5
25	Th	22 20 5	6 33 23	9 6	26 26 40	4 39	5 41	20 15	3♈13 59	3 S 11
26	F	22 24 1	7 33 43	8 44	10♈ 4 26	5 2	0 S 38	20 12	16 57 39	1 N56
27	S	22 27 58	8 34 1	8 22	23 53 14	5 8	4 N30	20 9	0♉50 51	7 2
28	☉	22 31 55	9♓34 18	7S 59	7♉50 7	4S 55	9 N28	20♋ 5	14♉50 46	11 N48

D M	Mercury		Venus		Mars		Jupiter	
	Lat.	Dec.	Lat.	Dec.	Lat.	Dec.	Lat.	Dec.
	° ′	° ′ ° ′	° ′	° ′ ° ′	° ′	° ′ ° ′	° ′	° ′
1	3 N32	13 S 55 14 S 11	7 N32	13 S 42 13 S 44	2 N50	4S 6 4S 10	1 N16	13 S 28
3	3 38	14 28 14 46	7 33	13 47 13 50	2 51	4 13 4 17	1 16	13 30
5	3 36	15 4 15 22	7 32	13 53 13 57	2 53	4 20 4 22	1 17	13 32
7	3 25	15 41 15 58	7 28	14 1 14 5	2 55	4 25 4 28	1 17	13 34
9	3 8	16 15 16 31	7 22	14 9 14 13	2 57	4 30 4 32	1 18	13 35
11	2 47	16 45 16 59	7 14	14 17 14 21	2 59	4 33 4 35	1 18	13 36
13	2 24	17 11 17 22	7 5	14 25 14 29	3 1	4 36 4 37	1 19	13 37
15	1 59	17 31 17 39	6 54	14 33 14 37	3 2	4 38 4 38	1 19	13 38
17	1 34	17 46 17 51	6 41	14 41 14 45	3 4	4 39 4 39	1 19	13 38
19	1 10	17 54 17 57	6 30	14 48 14 51	3 6	4 38 4 38	1 20	13 39
21	0 46	17 58 17 57	6 14	14 54 14 57	3 7	4 37 4 36	1 20	13 39
23	0 24	17 55 17 S 52	6 0	15 0 15S 2	3 9	4 35 4S 33	1 21	13 39
25	0 N 2	17 47	5 45	15 4	3 10	4 32	1 21	13 38
26	0 S 8	17 41	5 37	15 6	3 10	4 30	1 21	13 38
27	0 18	17 33	5 30	15 7	3 11	4 27	1 21	13 38
28	0 S 27	17 S 24	5 N22	15 S 8	3 N12	4 S 25	1 N22	13 S 37

First Quarter – February 1, 2h 28m pm (12° ♉ 25')

New Moon – February 8, 7*h* 57*m* *am (*19° ♌ *14')*

EPHEMERIS]			FEBRUARY, 1982														5
D	☿	♀	♂	♃	♄	♅	♆	♇	Lunar Aspects								
M	Long.	Long.	Long.	Long.	Long.	Long.	Long.	Long.	☉	☿	♀	♂	♃	♄	♅	♆	♇
	° ′	° ′	° ′	° ′	° ′	° ′	° ′	° ′									
1	11♒32	25♑10	17♎ 5	9♏32	22♎15	4♐ 2	26♐12	26♎56	□	□			☍			⚼	
2	10 ℞18	24 ℞48	17 17	9 36	22 ℞15	4 4	26 14	26 ℞56			△						
3	9 6	24 29	17 29	9 40	22 14	4 6	26 15	26 56	△	△	⚼	⚼		⚼	☍		⚼
4	7 57	24 12	17 40	9 43	22 14	4 8	26 17	26 55	⚼	⚼		△	⚼	△		☍	△
5	6 54	23 57	17 50	9 47	22 13	4 9	26 19	26 55					△				
6	5 56	23 45	18 0	9 50	22 13	4 11	26 20	26 55			☍	□		□	⚼		□
𝕾	5 6	23 36	18 9	9 53	22 12	4 13	26 22	26 55		☍			□		△	⚼	
8	4 24	23 29	18 18	9 56	22 11	4 14	26 23	26 54	☍			⚹		⚹		△	⚹
9	3 50	23 24	18 26	9 59	22 10	4 16	26 25	26 54			⚼	∠	⚹	∠	□		∠
10	3 25	23 22	18 33	10 2	22 9	4 17	26 26	26 53		⚼	△	⚺	∠	⚺			
11	3 7	23 D22	18 40	10 4	22 8	4 19	26 28	26 53	⚼	△					⚹	□	⚺
12	2 58	23 25	18 46	10 7	22 7	4 20	26 29	26 53				☌	⚺		∠		
13	2 D55	23 30	18 52	10 9	22 5	4 22	26 31	26 52	△	□	□			☌	⚺	⚹	☌
𝕾	3 0	23 38	18 56	10 11	22 4	4 23	26 32	26 51					☌			∠	
15	3 12	23 47	19 1	10 13	22 2	4 24	26 33	26 51	□		⚹	⚺		⚺		⚺	⚺
16	3 29	23 59	19 4	10 14	22 1	4 25	26 35	26 50		⚹	∠	∠	⚺	∠	☌		
17	3 53	24 13	19 7	10 15	21 59	4 26	26 36	26 50		∠		⚹		⚹			∠
18	4 22	24 29	19 9	10 17	21 57	4 27	26 37	26 49	⚹		⚺		∠			☌	⚹
19	4 56	24 47	19 10	10 18	21 55	4 28	26 39	26 48	∠	⚺			⚹		⚺		
20	5 34	25 8	19 11	10 18	21 53	4 29	26 40	26 48			☌	□		□	∠	⚺	□
𝕾	6 16	25 30	19 ℞11	10 19	21 51	4 30	26 41	26 47	⚺	☌			□		⚹		
22	7 3	25 53	19 10	10 19	21 49	4 31	26 42	26 46				△		△		∠	
23	7 53	26 19	19 8	10 20	21 47	4 32	26 43	26 45	☌		⚺	⚼			□	⚹	△
24	8 46	26 46	19 6	10 ℞20	21 44	4 33	26 44	26 44		⚺	∠		△	⚼			⚼
25	9 42	27 15	19 2	10 20	21 42	4 33	26 46	26 43		∠	⚹		⚼			□	
26	10 41	27 45	18 58	10 19	21 39	4 34	26 47	26 42	⚺	⚹					△		
27	11 43	28 17	18 54	10 19	21 36	4 35	26 48	26 41	∠		□	☍		☍	⚼	△	☍
𝕾	12♒47	28♑50	18♎48	10♏18	21♎34	4♐35	26♐49	26♎40	⚹	□			☍			⚼	

D	Saturn		Uranus		Neptune		Pluto	
M	Lat.	Dec.	Lat.	Dec.	Lat.	Dec.	Lat.	Dec.
	° ′	° ′	° ′	° ′	° ′	° ′	° ′	° ′
1	2 N34	6 S 17	0 N10	20 S 48	1 N16	22 S 7	17 N14	5 N43
3	2 35	6 16	0 10	20 48	1 16	22 8	17 15	5 44
5	2 35	6 15	0 10	20 49	1 16	22 8	17 16	5 46
7	2 36	6 14	0 10	20 49	1 16	22 8	17 17	5 47
9	2 36	6 13	0 10	20 50	1 16	22 8	17 18	5 48
11	2 37	6 12	0 10	20 51	1 16	22 8	17 19	5 49
13	2 37	6 10	0 10	20 51	1 16	22 8	17 20	5 51
15	2 38	6 8	0 10	20 52	1 16	22 8	17 21	5 52
17	2 38	6 7	0 10	20 52	1 16	22 8	17 22	5 53
19	2 39	6 5	0 10	20 52	1 16	22 8	17 23	5 55
21	2 39	6 3	0 10	20 53	1 16	22 8	17 24	5 56
23	2 40	6 1	0 10	20 53	1 16	22 8	17 25	5 58
25	2 40	5 59	0 10	20 53	1 16	22 8	17 26	5 59
26	2 41	5 57	0 10	20 53	1 16	22 8	17 27	6 0
27	2 41	5 56	0 10	20 54	1 16	22 8	17 27	6 1
28	2 N41	5 S 55	0 N10	20 S 54	1 N17	22 S 8	17 N28	6 N 1

Mutual Aspects

1. ☉ ☌ ☿. ☿ ∠ ♆.
3. ☿ □ ♃.
5. ☉ **Q** ♅.
6. ☉ **P** ☿.
7. ☉ △ ♂.
8. ☿ ⚹ ♅.
10. ☉ **P** ♀. ♀ **Stat.**
11. ☉ △ ♄.
12. ☉ ⚺ ♀, **P** ♃.
13. ☿ **Stat.**
15. ☉ ⚹ ♆, △ ♇.
18. ☿ ⚹ ♅.
19. ☉ ⊥ ♀.
20. ♂ **Stat.**
23. ☉ ⚼ ♂, □ ♅.
24. ♀ ⚺ ♆, □ ♇. ♃ **Stat.** ♆ ⚹ ♇.
25. ☉ ⚼ ♄. ♄ **P** ♇.
26. ☿ □ ♃.
27. ☉ **Q** ♆. ☿ ∠ ♆.

Last Quarter – February 15, 8*h* 21*m* *pm (*26° ♏*,50')*

TABLES OF HOUSES FOR LONDON, Latitude 51° 32′ N.

Upper band — Table 1

Sidereal Time H. M. S.	10 ♎	11 ♎	12 ♏	Ascen ♐	2 ♑	3 ♒
12 0 0	0	27	17	3 23	8	21
12 3 40	1	28	18	4 4	9	23
12 7 20	2	29	19	4 45	10	24
12 11 0	3	♏ 0	20	5 26	11	25
12 14 41	4	1	20	6 7	12	26
12 18 21	5	1	21	6 48	13	27
12 22 2	6	2	22	7 29	14	28
12 25 42	7	3	23	8 10	15	29
12 29 23	8	4	23	8 51	16	♓ 0
12 33 4	9	5	24	9 33	17	2
12 36 45	10	6	25	10 14	18	3
12 40 26	11	6	25	10 57	19	4
12 44 8	12	7	26	11 40	20	5
12 47 50	13	8	27	12 22	21	6
12 51 32	14	9	28	13 4	22	7
12 55 14	15	10	28	13 47	23	9
12 58 57	16	11	29	14 30	24	10
13 2 40	17	11	♐ 0	15 14	25	11
13 6 23	18	12	1	15 59	26	12
13 10 7	19	13	1	16 44	27	13
13 13 51	20	14	2	17 29	28	15
13 17 35	21	15	3	18 14	29	16
13 21 20	22	16	4	19 0	♒ 0	17
13 25 6	23	16	4	19 45	1	18
13 28 52	24	17	5	20 31	2	20
13 32 38	25	18	6	21 18	4	21
13 36 25	26	19	7	22 6	5	22
13 40 12	27	20	7	22 54	6	23
13 44 0	28	21	8	23 42	7	25
13 47 48	29	21	9	24 31	8	26
13 51 37	♏ 0	22	10	25 20	10	27

Upper band — Table 2

Sidereal Time H. M. S.	10 ♏	11 ♏	12 ♐	Ascen ♐	2 ♒	3 ♓
13 51 37	0	22	10	25 20	10	27
13 55 27	1	23	11	26 10	11	28
13 59 17	2	24	11	27 2	12	♈ 0
14 3 8	3	25	12	27 53	14	1
14 6 59	4	26	13	28 45	15	2
14 10 51	5	26	14	29 36	16	4
14 14 44	6	27	15	♑ 0 29	18	5
14 18 37	7	28	15	1 23	19	6
14 22 31	8	29	16	2 18	20	8
14 26 25	9	♐ 0?	17	3 14	22	9
14 30 20	10	1	18	4 11	23	10
14 34 16	11	2	19	5 9	25	11
14 38 13	12	2	20	6 7	26	13
14 42 10	13	3	20	6 28	14	16
14 46 8	14	4	21	8 6	29	15
14 50 7	15	5	22	9 8	♓ 0	17
14 54 7	16	6	23	10 11	2	18
14 58 7	17	7	24	11 15	4	19
15 2 8	18	8	25	12 20	5	21
15 6 9	19	9	26	13 27	6	22
15 10 12	20	10	27	14 35	9	23
15 14 15	21	10	27	15 43	11	24
15 18 19	22	11	28	16 52	13	26
15 22 23	23	12	29	18 3	14	27
15 26 29	24	13	♑ 0	19 16	16	28
15 30 35	25	14	1	20 32	17	29
15 34 41	26	15	2	21 49	19	♉ 0
15 38 49	27	16	3	23 8	21	1
15 42 57	28	17	4	24 28	22	2
15 47 6	29	18	5	25 51	24	3
15 51 15	♐ 0	18	6	27 15	26	6

Upper band — Table 3

Sidereal Time H. M. S.	10 ♐	11 ♐	12 ♑	Ascen ♑	2 ♓	3 ♉
15 51 15	0	18	6	27 15	26	6
15 55 25	1	19	7	28 42	28	7
15 59 36	2	20	8	♒ 0 11	♈ 0	9
16 3 48	3	21	9	1 42	2	10
16 8 0	4	22	10	3 16	3	11
16 12 13	5	23	11	4 53	5	12
16 16 26	6	24	12	6 32	7	14
16 20 40	7	25	13	8 13	9	15
16 24 55	8	26	14	9 57	11	16
16 29 10	9	27	16	11 44	12	17
16 33 26	10	28	17	13 34	14	18
16 37 42	11	29	18	15 26	16	20
16 41 59	12	♑	19	17 20	18	21
16 46 16	13	1	20	19 18	20	22
16 50 34	14	2	21	21 21	22	23
16 54 52	15	3	22	23 29	25	25
16 59 10	16	4	24	25 36	26	26
17 3 29	17	5	25	27 46	♈ 0	28
17 7 49	18	6	26	♓ 0 28	2	♊
17 12 9	19	7	27	2 19	8	29
17 16 29	20	8	29	4 40	2	♊
17 20 49	21	9	♒ 0	7 2	3	1
17 25 9	22	10	1	9 26	5	2
17 29 30	23	11	3	11 54	7	3
17 33 51	24	12	4	14 24	8	5
17 38 12	25	13	5	17 0	10	6
17 42 34	26	14	7	19 33	11	7
17 46 55	27	15	8	22 6	13	8
17 51 17	28	16	10	24 40	14	9
17 55 38	29	17	11	27 27	16	10
18 0 0	♑ 0	18	13	0 ♈ 0	18	11

Lower band — Table 1

Sidereal Time H. M. S.	10 ♑	11 ♑	12 ♒	Ascen ♈	2 ♉	3 ♊
18 0 0	0	18	13	0 17	11	20
18 4 22	1	20	14	2 39	13	21
18 8 43	2	21	16	5 19	14	22
18 13 5	3	22	17	7 55	16	23
18 17 26	4	23	19	10 29	18	25
18 21 48	5	24	20	13	19	26
18 26 9	6	25	22	15 36	20	27
18 30 30	7	26	23	18 6	22	29
18 34 51	8	27	25	20 41	24	♋
18 39 11	9	29	27	22 59	25	1
18 43 31	10	♒ 0	28	25 22	27	2
18 47 51	11	1	♓ 0	27 42	28	3
18 52 11	12	2	2	29 58	♊ 0	4
18 56 31	13	3	3	2 ♉ 13	1	5
19 0 50	14	4	5	4 24	3	6
19 5 8	15	6	7	6 30	5	8
19 9 26	16	7	8	8 36	6	9
19 13 44	17	8	10	10 40	8	10
19 18 1	18	9	12	12 39	9	11
19 22 18	19	10	14	14 35	11	12
19 26 34	20	12	16	16 28	13	13
19 30 50	21	13	18	18 17	14	14
19 35 5	22	14	20	20 3	16	16
19 39 20	23	15	21	21 45	17	17
19 43 34	24	16	23	23 25	18	18
19 47 47	25	18	25	25 9	19	19
19 52 0	26	19	27	26 19	21	20
19 56 12	27	20	28	28 18	21	22
20 0 24	28	21	♈ 0	29 49	22	23
20 4 35	29	23	2	1 ♊ 11	23	24
20 8 45	30	24	4	2 45	24	12

Lower band — Table 2

Sidereal Time H. M. S.	10 ♒	11 ♒	12 ♈	Ascen ♉	2 ♊	3 ♋
20 8 45	0	24	4	2 45	24	12
20 12 54	1	25	6	4 9	25	12
20 17 3	2	27	7	5 32	26	13
20 21 11	3	28	9	6 53	27	14
20 25 19	4	29	11	8 12	28	15
20 29 26	5	♓ 0	13	9 29	29	16
20 33 31	6	2	14	10 43	♋ 0	17
20 37 37	7	3	16	11 58	1	18
20 41 41	8	4	18	13 9	2	19
20 45 45	9	6	19	14 18	3	20
20 49 48	10	7	21	15 25	3	21
20 53 51	11	9	23	16 32	4	21
20 57 52	12	9	24	17 39	5	22
21 1 53	13	11	26	18 44	6	23
21 5 53	14	13	29	19 48	7	24
21 9 53	15	13	♉ 0	20 51	8	25
21 13 52	16	15	2	21 50	9	26
21 17 50	17	16	4	22 47	9	27
21 21 47	18	17	6	23 44	10	28
21 25 44	19	19	8	24 39	11	29
21 29 40	20	20	9	25 33	12	♌
21 33 35	21	22	11	26 25	13	1
21 37 29	22	23	12	27 16	14	2
21 41 23	23	24	14	28 8	15	3
21 45 16	24	26	16	29 15	16	4
21 49 9	25	26	16	0 ♊ 22	16	4
21 53 1	26	19	18	1 26	15	17
21 56 52	27	29	16	2 7	18	5
22 0 43	28	♈ 20	18	43 28	19	6
22 4 33	29	1	19	4 33	19	7
22 8 23	30	3	20	4 38	20	8

Lower band — Table 3

Sidereal Time H. M. S.	10 ♓	11 ♈	12 ♉	Ascen ♊	2 ♋	3 ♌
22 8 23	0	3	20	4 38	20	8
22 12 12	1	4	21	5 28	21	8
22 16 0	2	6	23	6 23	22	9
22 19 48	3	7	24	7 24	23	10
22 23 35	4	8	25	7 53	23	11
22 27 22	5	9	26	9 26	24	12
22 31 8	6	10	28	9 25	25	14
22 34 54	7	12	29	10 16	26	14
22 38 40	8	13	♊	11 11	26	15
22 42 25	9	14	1	11 47	27	15
22 46 9	10	15	2	7 16	11	16
22 49 53	11	17	3	13 3	18	17
22 53 37	12	18	4	14 1	29	18
22 57 20	13	19	5	14 45	♌ 0	19
23 1 3	14	20	6	15 28	1	19
23 4 46	15	21	7	16 11	1	20
23 8 28	16	23	8	16 53	2	21
23 12 10	17	24	9	17 37	3	22
23 15 52	18	25	10	18 20	4	23
23 19 34	19	26	11	19 1	5	24
23 23 15	20	27	12	19 45	5	24
23 26 56	21	29	13	20 27	6	25
23 30 37	22	♉	14	21 8	7	26
23 34 18	23	1	15	21 50	7	27
23 37 58	24	2	16	22 31	8	28
23 41 39	25	3	17	23 12	9	28
23 45 12	26	4	18	23 52	10	29
23 49 0	27	5	19	24 32	10	♍
23 52 46	28	6	20	25 12	11	1
23 56 20	29	8	21	25 50	12	2
24 0 0	♈ 0	9	22	26 36	13	3

TABLES OF HOUSES FOR LIVERPOOL, Latitude 53° 25′ N.

Upper table

Sidereal Time H. M. S.	10 ≏	11 ≏	12 ♏	Ascen ♐ ° ′	2 ♑	3 ♒
12 0 0	0	27	16	1 48	6	21
12 3 40	1	28	17	2 27	7	22
12 7 20	2	29	18	3 6	8	23
12 11 0	3	♏	18	3 46	9	24
12 14 41	4	0	19	4 25	10	25
12 18 21	5	1	20	5 6	10	26
12 22 2	6	2	21	5 46	11	28
12 25 42	7	3	21	6 26	12	29
12 29 23	8	4	22	7 6	13	♓
12 33 4	9	4	23	7 46	14	1
12 36 45	10	5	24	8 27	15	2
12 40 26	11	6	24	9 8	16	3
12 44 8	12	7	25	9 49	17	5
12 47 50	13	8	26	10 30	18	6
12 51 32	14	9	26	11 12	19	7
12 55 14	15	9	27	11 54	20	8
12 58 57	16	10	28	12 36	21	10
13 2 40	17	11	28	13 19	22	11
13 6 23	18	12	29	14 2	23	12
13 10 7	19	13	♐	14 45	25	13
13 13 51	20	13	1	15 28	26	15
13 17 35	21	14	1	16 12	27	16
13 21 20	22	15	2	16 56	28	17
13 25 6	23	16	3	17 41	29	18
13 28 52	24	17	4	18 26	≈	19
13 32 38	25	17	4	19 11	1	21
13 36 25	26	18	5	19 57	3	22
13 40 12	27	19	6	20 44	4	23
13 44 0	28	20	7	21 31	5	24
13 47 48	29	21	7	22 18	7	26
13 51 37	30	21	8	23 6	8	27

Sidereal Time H. M. S.	10 ♏	11 ♏	12 ♐	Ascen ♐ ° ′	2 ≈	3 ♓
13 51 37	0	21	8	23 6	8	27
13 55 27	1	22	9	23 55	9	28
13 59 17	2	23	10	24 43	10	♈
14 3 8	3	24	10	25 33	12	1
14 6 50	4	25	11	26 23	13	2
14 10 51	5	26	12	27 14	15	4
14 14 44	6	26	13	28 6	16	5
14 18 37	7	27	13	28 59	18	6
14 22 31	8	28	14	29 52	19	8
14 26 25	9	29	15	0 ♑ 46	20	9
14 30 20	10	♐	16	1 41	22	10
14 34 16	11	1	17	2 36	23	11
14 38 13	12	2	18	3 33	25	13
14 42 10	13	2	18	4 30	26	14
14 46 8	14	3	19	5 29	28	16
14 50 7	15	4	20	6 29	♓	17
14 54 7	16	5	21	7 30	1	18
14 58 7	17	6	22	8 32	3	20
15 2 8	18	7	23	9 35	5	21
15 6 9	19	8	24	10 39	6	22
15 10 12	20	8	24	11 45	8	23
15 14 15	21	9	25	12 52	10	25
15 18 19	22	10	26	14 1	11	26
15 22 23	23	11	27	15 11	13	27
15 26 29	24	12	28	16 23	15	29
15 30 35	25	13	29	17 37	17	♈
15 34 41	26	14	♑	18 53	19	1
15 38 49	27	15	1	20 10	21	3
15 42 57	28	16	2	21 29	22	4
15 47 6	29	17	2	22 51	24	5
15 51 15	30	17	3	24 15	26	7

Sidereal Time H. M. S.	10 ♐	11 ♐	12 ♑	Ascen ♑ ° ′	2 ♓	3 ♉
15 51 15	0	17	4	24 15	26	7
15 55 25	1	18	5	25 41	28	8
15 59 36	2	19	6	27 10	♈	9
16 3 48	3	20	7	28 41	2	10
16 8 0	4	21	8	0 ≈ 14	4	12
16 12 13	5	22	9	1 50	5	13
16 16 26	6	23	10	3 30	7	14
16 20 40	7	24	11	5 13	9	15
16 24 55	8	25	12	6 58	11	17
16 29 10	9	26	13	8 46	13	18
16 33 26	10	27	14	10 38	15	19
16 37 42	11	28	15	12 32	17	20
16 41 59	12	29	16	14 31	19	22
16 46 16	13	♑	18	16 33	20	23
16 50 34	14	1	19	18 40	22	24
16 54 52	15	2	20	20 50	24	26
16 59 10	16	3	21	23 4	26	26
17 3 29	17	4	22	25 21	28	28
17 7 49	18	5	24	27 42	29	29
17 12 9	19	6	25	0 ♈ 8	♉	♊
17 16 29	20	7	26	2 37	3	1
17 20 49	21	8	28	5 10	5	3
17 25 9	22	9	29	7 46	6	4
17 29 30	23	11	≈	10 24	8	5
17 33 51	24	12	1	13 6	10	6
17 37 ...	25	13	...	...	...	7
17 42 ...	26	14	...	...	...	9
17 46 55	27	14	6	21 ...	...	9
17 51 ...	29	16	7	24 ...	...	12
17 55 38	29	16	9	27 ...	...	12
18 0 0	30	17	11	0 30	...	13

Lower table

Sidereal Time H. M. S.	10 ♑	11 ♑	12 ≈	Ascen ♈ ° ′	2 ♉	3 ♊
18 0 0	0	17	11	0 0	19	13
18 4 22	1	18	12	2 52	21	14
18 8 43	2	20	14	5 43	23	15
18 13 5	3	21	16	8 33	24	16
18 17 26	4	22	17	11 22	25	17
18 21 48	5	23	19	14 8	27	18
18 26 9	6	24	20	16 53	28	19
18 30 30	7	25	22	19 36	♊	20
18 34 51	8	26	24	22 14	1	21
18 39 11	9	27	25	24 50	2	22
18 43 31	10	29	27	27 22	4	23
18 47 51	11	≈	28	29 52	5	24
18 52 11	12	1	♓	2 ♉ 18	6	25
18 56 31	13	2	2	4 39	8	26
19 0 50	14	4	4	6 56	9	27
19 5 8	15	5	6	9 10	10	28
19 9 26	16	6	8	11 20	11	29
19 13 44	17	7	10	13 27	12	♋
19 18 1	18	8	11	15 29	14	1
19 22 18	19	9	13	17 28	15	2
19 26 34	20	11	15	19 40	16	3
19 30 50	21	12	17	21 14	17	4
19 35 5	22	13	19	23 2	18	5
19 39 20	23	15	21	24 47	19	6
19 43 34	24	16	23	26 30	20	7
19 47 47	25	17	25	28 10	21	8
19 52 0	26	18	26	29 46	22	9
19 56 12	27	20	28	1 ♊ 22	23	10
20 0 24	28	21	♈	2 50	24	11
20 4 35	29	22	2	4 19	25	12
20 8 45	30	23	4	5 45	26	13

Sidereal Time H. M. S.	10 ≈	11 ≈	12 ♈	Ascen ♊ ° ′	2 ♊	3 ♋
18 0 0	0	23	4	5 45	26	13
18 4 22	1	25	6	7 9	27	14
18 8 43	2	26	8	8 31	28	14
18 13 5	3	27	9	9 50	29	15
18 17 26	4	29	11	11 7	♋	16
18 21 48	5	♓	13	12 23	1	17
18 26 9	6	1	15	13 37	2	18
18 30 30	7	3	17	14 49	3	19
18 34 51	8	4	19	16 1	4	19
18 39 11	9	5	20	17 8	5	20
18 43 31	10	7	22	18 15	6	21
18 47 51	11	8	24	19 21	7	22
18 52 11	12	9	25	20 25	7	23
18 56 31	13	11	27	21 31	8	24
19 0 50	14	12	29	21 53	9	25
19 5 8	15	13	♉	23 8	10	25
19 9 26	16	14	2	24 4	11	26
19 13 44	17	16	4	25 2	12	27
19 18 1	18	17	6	25 58	13	28
19 22 18	19	18	7	26 54	14	29
19 26 34	20	20	9	27 48	15	Ω
19 30 50	21	21	10	28 42	16	1
19 35 5	22	22	12	29 34	17	2
19 39 20	23	24	14	0 ♋ 27	18	3
19 43 34	24	25	16	1 17	19	4
19 47 47	25	27	18	2 8	20	4
19 52 0	26	28	19	2 58	20	5
19 56 12	27	♈	21	3 52	21	6
20 0 24	28	1	23	4 40	22	7
20 4 35	29	2	25	5 28	23	8
20 8 45	30	3	26	6 19	24	9

Sidereal Time H. M. S.	10 ♓	11 ♈	12 ♉	Ascen ♋ ° ′	2 ♋	3 Ω
18 0 0	0	3	22	6 54	22	8
18 4 22	1	4	23	7 42	23	9
18 8 43	2	5	25	8 29	23	10
18 13 5	3	7	26	9 16	24	11
18 17 26	4	8	27	10 3	25	12
18 21 48	5	9	29	10 49	26	13
18 26 9	6	11	♊	11 34	26	13
18 30 30	7	12	2	12 19	27	14
18 34 51	8	13	3	13 3	28	15
18 39 11	9	15	5	13 48	29	16
18 43 31	10	16	6	14 32	Ω	17
18 47 51	11	17	8	15 15	1	17
18 52 11	12	18	9	15 58	1	18
18 56 31	13	20	11	16 41	2	19
19 0 50	14	21	12	17 24	3	20
19 5 8	15	22	13	18 6	3	21
19 9 26	16	23	15	18 48	4	21
19 13 44	17	25	16	19 30	4	22
19 18 1	18	26	18	20 11	5	23
19 22 18	19	28	20	20 52	6	24
19 26 34	20	29	21	21 33	6	25
19 30 50	21	♉	23	22 14	7	26
19 35 5	22	2	24	22 54	8	26
19 39 20	23	3	26	23 34	8	27
19 43 34	24	5	27	24 14	9	28
19 47 47	25	6	29	24 54	10	29
19 52 0	26	8	♊	25 35	11	♍
19 56 12	27	9	2	26 14	11	1
20 0 24	28	11	3	26 54	12	1
20 4 35	29	12	5	27 33	13	2
20 8 45	30	14	6	28 12	14	3

TABLES OF HOUSES FOR NEW YORK, Latitude 40° 43′ N.

Sidereal Time	10 ♎	11 ♎	12 ♏	Ascen ♐	2 ♑	3 ♒	Sidereal Time	10 ♏	11 ♏	12 ♐	Ascen ♑	2 ♒	3 ♓	Sidereal Time	10 ♐	11 ♐	12 ♑	Ascen ♒	2 ♓	3 ♉
H. M. S.	°	°	°	° ′	°	°	H. M. S.	°	°	°	° ′	°	°	H. M. S.	°	°	°	° ′	°	°
12 0 0	0	29	21	11 7	15	24	13 51 37	0	25	15	5 35	16	27	15 51 15	0	21	13	9 8	27	4
12 3 40	1	♏	22	11 52	16	25	13 55 27	1	25	16	6 30	17	29	15 55 25	1	22	14	10 31	28	5
12 7 20	2	1	23	12 37	17	26	13 59 17	2	26	17	7 27	18	♈	15 59 36	2	23	15	11 56	♈	6
12 11 0	3	1	24	13 19	17	27	14 3 8	3	27	18	8 23	20	1	16 3 48	3	24	16	13 23	1	7
12 14 41	4	2	25	14 7	18	28	14 6 59	4	28	18	9 20	21	2	16 8 0	4	25	17	14 50	3	9
12 18 21	5	3	25	14 52	19	29	14 10 51	5	29	19	10 17	22	4	16 12 13	5	26	18	16 19	4	10
12 22 2	6	4	26	15 38	20	♓	14 14 44	6	♐	20	11 16	23	5	16 16 26	6	27	19	17 50	6	11
12 25 42	7	5	27	16 23	21	1	14 18 37	7	1	21	12 15	24	6	16 20 19	7	28	20	19 22	7	12
12 29 23	8	6	28	17 11	22	2	14 22 31	8	2	22	13 14	25	8	16 24 55	8	29	21	20 56	9	13
12 33 4	9	6	28	17 58	23	3	14 26 25	9	2	23	14 15	27	9	16 29 10	9	♑	22	22 30	11	15
12 36 45	10	7	29	18 45	24	4	14 30 20	10	3	24	15 16	28	10	16 33 20	10	1	23	24 7	12	16
12 40 26	11	8	♐	19 32	25	5	14 34 16	11	4	24	16 17	29	11	16 37 42	11	2	24	25 44	14	17
12 44 8	12	9	1	20 20	26	7	14 38 13	12	5	25	17 18	♈	13	16 41 59	12	3	26	27 23	15	18
12 47 50	13	10	2	21 8	27	8	14 42 10	13	6	26	18 19	1	14	16 46 16	13	4	27	29 4	17	19
12 51 32	14	11	2	21 57	28	9	14 46 8	14	7	27	19 21	2	16	16 50 34	14	5	28	0♒45	18	20
12 55 14	15	12	3	22 43	29	10	14 50 7	15	8	28	20 24	4	17	16 54 52	15	6	29	2 29	20	22
12 58 57	16	13	4	23 33	≈	11	14 54 7	16	9	29	21 27	5	18	16 59 10	16	7	≈	4 11	21	23
13 2 40	17	13	5	24 22	1	12	14 58 7	17	10	♑	22 31	7	20	17 3 29	17	8	2	5 56	23	24
13 6 23	18	14	6	25 11	2	13	15 2 8	18	10	1	23 35	8	21	17 7 49	18	9	3	7 43	24	25
13 10 7	19	15	7	26 1	3	15	15 6 9	19	11	2	24 40	9	23	17 12 9	19	10	4	9 30	26	26
13 13 51	20	16	7	26 50	5	16	15 10 12	20	12	3	25 46	11	24	17 16 29	20	11	5	11 18	27	28
13 17 35	21	17	8	27 40	6	17	15 14 15	21	13	4	26 52	12	25	17 20 49	21	12	7	13 8	29	28
13 21 20	22	18	9	28 32	7	18	15 18 19	22	14	5	28 0	14	27	17 25 9	22	13	8	14 57	♉	1
13 25 6	23	19	10	29 23	8	19	15 22 23	23	15	6	29 9	15	28	17 29 23	23	14	9	16 48	1	2
13 28 52	24	19	10	0♑14	9	20	15 26 29	24	16	6	0≈20	17	29	17 33 51	24	15	10	18 41	3	2
13 32 38	25	20	11	1 7	10	21	15 30 35	25	16	7	1 33	18	♉	17 38 12	25	16	12	20 33	5	4
13 36 25	26	21	12	2 0	11	23	15 34 41	26	17	8	2 49	19	1	17 42 34	26	17	13	22 25	6	5
13 40 12	27	22	13	2 52	12	24	15 38 49	27	18	9	4 6	21	2	17 46 55	27	19	14	24 19	7	6
13 44 0	28	23	13	3 46	13	25	15 42 57	28	19	10	5 25	22	3	17 51 17	28	20	16	26 12	9	6
13 47 48	29	24	14	4 41	15	26	15 47 6	29	21	11	6 45	23	5	17 55 38	29	21	17	28 7	10	7
—	—	—	—	—	—	—	15 51 15	0	25	15	—	—	—	18 0 0	0	30	18	0♊30	12	8

Sidereal Time	10 ♑	11 ♑	12 ♒	Ascen ♈	2 ♉	3 ♊	Sidereal Time	10 ♒	11 ♒	12 ♈	Ascen ♉	2 ♊	3 ♋	Sidereal Time	10 ♓	11 ♈	12 ♉	Ascen ♊	2 ♋	3 ♌
H. M. S.	°	°	°	° ′	°	°	H. M. S.	°	°	°	° ′	°	°	H. M. S.	°	°	°	° ′	°	°
18 0 0	0	22	18	0 0	12	9	20 8 45	0	8	26	3 20	17	9	22 8 23	0	3	14	24 25	15	5
18 4 22	1	23	20	0 53	13	10	20 12 54	1	27	5	22 14	18	10	22 12 12	1	4	15	25 19	16	6
18 8 43	2	24	21	1 48	14	11	20 17 3	2	29	6	23 9	19	11	22 16 0	2	5	17	26 14	17	7
18 13 5	3	25	23	2 41	16	12	20 21 11	3	♈	8	24 8	21	12	22 19 48	3	6	18	27 8	17	8
18 17 26	4	26	24	3 35	17	13	20 25 19	4	1	9	25 0	22	13	22 23 35	4	7	19	28 0	18	9
18 21 48	5	27	25	4 27	18	14	20 29 30	5	2	11	25 52	23	14	22 27 22	5	8	20	28 53	19	10
18 26 9	6	28	27	5 19	20	15	20 33 31	6	3	12	28 47	23	14	22 31 8	6	10	21	29 46	20	11
18 30 30	7	29	28	6 12	21	16	20 37 37	7	5	13	0♊11	24	15	22 34 54	7	11	22	0♋37	21	11
18 34 51	8	≈	♈	7 6	22	17	20 41 41	8	6	15	1 17	25	16	22 38 40	8	12	23	1 28	21	12
18 39 11	9	2	1	7 57	24	18	20 45 45	9	7	16	2 9	26	17	22 42 25	9	13	24	2 20	22	13
18 43 31	10	3	3	8 49	25	19	20 49 48	10	8	18	3 8	27	18	22 46 9	10	14	25	3 9	23	14
18 47 51	11	4	4	9 40	26	20	20 53 51	11	9	19	4 0	28	19	22 49 53	11	15	27	3 59	24	15
18 52 11	12	5	5	10 32	28	21	20 57 52	12	10	20	4 59	29	20	22 53 37	12	17	28	4 49	24	16
18 56 31	13	6	7	11 23	29	22	21 1 53	13	12	22	5 53	♋	21	22 57 20	13	18	29	5 38	25	17
19 0 0	14	7	8	12 15	♊	23	21 5 53	14	13	23	6 52	1	22	23 1 3	14	19	♋	6 27	26	18
19 5 8	15	9	10	13 6	2	24	21 9 53	15	14	25	7 46	2	23	23 4 46	15	20	1	7 17	27	18
19 9 26	16	10	12	13 52	3	25	21 13 52	16	15	26	8 41	3	24	23 8 28	16	21	2	8 3	28	19
19 13 44	17	11	13	14 47	5	26	21 17 50	17	16	28	9 35	4	25	23 12 10	17	23	4	8 52	29	20
19 18 1	18	12	15	15 37	6	27	21 21 47	18	18	29	10 29	5	26	23 15 52	18	24	5	9 40	♌	21
19 22 18	19	13	16	16 28	8	28	21 25 44	19	19	♉	11 23	6	27	23 19 34	19	25	6	10 28	♌	22
19 26 34	20	14	18	17 20	9	29	21 29 40	20	21	2	12 14	7	28	23 23 15	20	26	7	11 15	1	23
19 30 50	21	15	19	18 11	11	♋	21 33 35	21	22	3	13 15	8	29	23 26 56	21	27	8	12 2	2	24
19 35 5	22	16	21	19 2	12	1	21 37 29	22	23	5	14 5	9	♌	23 30 50	22	28	9	12 49	3	25
19 39 20	23	18	22	19 52	13	2	21 41 23	23	24	6	15 6	10	1	23 34 18	23	29	10	13 37	3	25
19 43 34	24	19	24	20 43	15	3	21 45 16	24	25	7	16 4	11	2	23 37 58	24	♉	11	14 24	4	26
19 47 47	25	20	25	21 34	16	4	21 49 9	25	27	8	19 8	12	3	23 41 39	25	1	13	15 8	5	27
19 52 0	26	21	27	22 25	18	5	21 53 1	26	28	9	20 2	12	4	23 45 19	26	2	15	53	5	28
19 56 12	27	22	28	23 16	19	6	21 56 52	27	29	11	20 43	13	5	23 49 0	27	3	16	41	6	28
20 0 24	28	24	♈	24 6	20	7	22 0 43	28	♈	12	21 22	13	5	23 52 40	28	4	17	23	7	29
20 4 35	29	25	2	24 57	22	8	22 4 33	29	1	13	23 30	14	5	23 56 20	29	5	18	8	8	♍
20 8 45	0	26	3	25 47	23	9	22 8 23	0	3	14	24 25	15	5	24 0 0	0	6	18	53	9	1

Useful Addresses

Astrological stationery, chart forms and ephemerids are available from the following suppliers:

W Foulsham & Co Ltd, Yeovil Road, Slough, Berks SL1 4JH. Tel: 0753 26769 (ephemerides for all years)
L N Fowler & Co. Ltd, 1201, High Road, Chadwell Heath, Romford, Essex RM6 4DH
Compendium Bookshop, 234 Camden High Street, London NWI
Mysteries, 9 Monmouth Street, London WC2
W & G Foyle Limited, 119 Charing Cross Road, London WC2
Watkins Books Limited, 21 Cecil Court, London WC2

AUSTRALIA

Federation of
Australian
Astrologers
Lynda Hill
20 Harley Road
Avalon
NSW 2107
Tel: + 61-2-918-9539

USA

American
Federation of
Astrologers
Robert Cooper
Executive Secretary
PO Box 22040
Tempe (check this)
42 85285-2040
Tel: 602-838-1751
Fax: 602-838-8293

NEW ZEALAND

Astrological Society
of New Zealand
Joy Dowler
President
5266 Wellesley
Street
Auckland 1003

INDEX